Also by Brooke Astor

The Last Blossom on the Plum Tree

Footprints: An Autobiography

The Bluebird Is at Home

PATCHWORK CHILD

RANDOM HOUSE  NEW YORK

Brooke asTor

PATCHWORK CHILD ✿ EARLY MEMORIES

IN MEMORY OF MY MOTHER AND FATHER

Library of Congress Cataloging-in-Publication Data

Astor, Brooke.
Patchwork child : early memories / Brooke Astor.—1st ed.
p.   cm.
Summary: Brooke Astor's memoir of her childhood years in Hawaii,
Panama, Peking, Santo Domingo, and turn-of-the-century Washington, D.C.
ISBN 0-679-42687-6
1. Astor, Brooke—Biography—Youth.   2. Novelists, American—20th
century —Biography.   [1. Astor, Brooke.   2. Authors, American.]
I. Title.
PS3551.S68Z47   1992
813'.54—dc20
[B]   93-12953

Manufactured in the United States of America
24689753
Random House, Inc. 1993 Edition

ACKNOWLEDGMENTS

I especially wish to thank my editor, Jason Epstein, whose idea it was to do this book, and the following people, without whose inspiration and help and dedication this book could never have been published: Rochelle Udell and Mary Maguire of Condé Nast Publications; Gail Garcia, design/computer production; Kathy Rosenbloom, director of production, Random House; Sono Rosenberg, copy editor, Random House; Sarah Parr, Condé Nast assistant; and Mallay Charters, Random House assistant.

CONTENTS

PREFACE TO THE NEW EDITION
PAGE XI

1
INTRODUCTION TO THE PATCHWORK
PAGE 3

2
HOWARDS AND MARINES
AND FIRST DUTY IN HAWAII
PAGE 13

3
PANAMA: RED DUST, MOSQUITOES, AND ROSES
(AND A MAD DOG)
PAGE 23

4
"IF THE DAY IT HAD BEEN FINER..."
PAGE 32

5
PEKING PAGEANTRY
PAGE 42

6
A WORM'S-EYE VIEW OF LIFE
PAGE 56

7
PARTIES, PARTIES, PARTIES
PAGE 76

8
"THE SURPRISE"
PAGE 97

9
MABEL AND JOHN
PAGE 110

10

THE TEMPLE OF ONE HUNDRED COURTYARDS

PAGE 123

11

THE MIRACLE

PAGE 135

12

THE PAINS OF GROWING UP

PAGE 143

13

GROWN-UPS ARE BEST IN THE DRAWING ROOM

PAGE 173

14

MORTON

PAGE 194

15

LIEUTENANTS AND CARIBBEAN MOONLIGHT

PAGE 213

16

INCARCERATION

PAGE 230

17

THE PROM

PAGE 243

18

A FAMILY NOTE

PAGE 255

EPILOGUE

PAGE 262

Preface
to the
New Edition

When my memoir *Footprints* was published in 1981, I received many letters from people saying that the book had meant much to them because of the philosophy they had found in it. I was surprised by that, as I had written what I thought was a very straightforward, simple account of my life from the age of sixteen until the death of my husband, Vincent, in 1959. I was naturally very pleased by these comments and I put the letters safely away in a large folder. That was twelve years ago. Since then, I have written a novel and many articles.

I had, however, written an earlier memoir, this one about my childhood. It was called *Patchwork Child* and was published in 1961. It had a certain success, but it is now out of print. It was only recently, when my editor came to visit me in Maine, that he suggested republishing it with many more photographs than in the original version and any additional comments that might occur to me. I began to think it over, wondering just what more I could say, but as I read it I began to realize that *Patchwork Child* described the foundation of my character and approach to life. It made me realize how tremendously important one's childhood is. It forms one's character and outlook and philosophy. The Jesuits are supposed to say, "Give me a child until he is seven and he will be ready to face life."

As I look back, the two things that have helped me most have been an undying love of reading and my love of nature. Because of this, I have been able to survive—my marriage at seventeen to a flagrantly unfaithful, drunken husband, who knocked me down and broke my jaw when I was six months pregnant; the death of my adored second husband, who dropped dead beside me on Thanksgiving night; and my third husband's death, after only five and a half years of marriage. Vincent was not an easy man. He had had an unhappy childhood and, unlike me, was insecure and not at ease with people. I think I made him happy. At least he told me so, and he left me the Vincent Astor Foundation, which has been my life ever since—and has given me enormous pleasure in being able to help others.

I am forever grateful to my parents. They were not at all alike

(previous page)
*Uncle Charlie and Grand-
father with me on N Street*

in character, but they loved each other and they loved me. To be a loved and an only child, is a gift of God. All of my parents' love and intelligence nourished me and prepared me for the future.

Mother lived on curiosity . . . curiosity about everything—books, art, music, ballet—she was constantly involved in something interesting and tried to pass her spirited approach to life on to me. "Don't just read any book," she would say. "You must read something that gives you a different view of life. Read something that opens a door—even if you do not quite understand it at the time—you will later—and it will help you." This was rather heady advice to give a girl of twelve. I had already read some Dickens, Thackeray, and Jane Austen, but I then began to branch out into Chekhov, Dostoyevski, Walter Pater, Flaubert, Stendhal, Dumas, Henry Adams, and thanks to Mother, I also had heard Sarah Bernhardt lecture and recite, and seen Nijinsky leap through the window in *Le Spectre de la Rose*. This was combined with keyhole listenings to Mother and her best friend discussing the charms of the sculptor Gutzon Borglum and the beauty of the memorial to Henry Adams's wife by Saint-Gaudens. Such delicious glimpses of the Grown-up world made me, starting at about twelve, take a view of life and report on it in my writings and little sketches. I, in fact, remained in total ignorance of real life and especially of sex. It seems incredible in these days, but I was as ignorant as a babe of two weeks when, at just seventeen, I married. A worldly friend of mine, at the age of fourteen, had tried to explain the facts of life to me, but I cut her off, saying haughtily, "My father and mother would never do things like that." But in spite of all this, I survived my marriage, though the marriage itself didn't survive.

To get back to my very early childhood, Father was on duty with the Marine Corps in the Far East until I was three, and Mother and I were living at my grandparents' home in Washington, D.C. But when Father came home he was soon ordered out to Hawaii. I was only three and a half at the time and thus introduced to an entirely different life.

After that we went to Panama, where my father was in charge

*Mabel and John Russell
(1901) on their honeymoon
at Niagara Falls*

of guarding the Canal, which was being built at that time. There I was taught to ride, and I had a wonderful time. It was extremely hot, and the only flowers that seemed to grow well there were roses. I used to sit under the rosebushes and ruminate about the future. Mother disliked Panama, even though Colonel Goethals (later General), who was in charge of constructing the Canal, built a special indoor patio for her. Still, she was unhappy and some of her unhappiness touched me. I know Father enjoyed Panama until he was bitten by a mad dog and we had to return quickly to the United States. Then, oh joy (for Mother), we were stationed in Newport, Rhode Island.

Father was sent to Newport to teach at the U.S. Navy War College and we were there almost two years. I was nearly six and so I was sent to school. By then I could already read and write quite well. In fact, I was writing poetry, so that when we went to Peking in 1909 (when I was just seven), Father said, as we went up the Yangtze River, "If you can learn to speak Chinese, you can have any type of pet that you want," and Mother said, "If you keep a diary, I will read to you every day." I must inject something very important here, and that is that my parents had a marvelous sense of humor and we three could laugh together at almost everything, including ourselves.

China made the greatest impression on my life and very much on my inner spirit. First of all, my family was extremely busy—Father with his fellow officers from other legations and Mother with her very fascinating social life with sophisticated, intelligent, amusing people from all the European nations. As a child, I watched everything that they did, including things that I could not understand.

For my parents, living in Peking was about as glamorous, sophisticated, and interesting a life as one could find anywhere. They were out every night. French was the language in those days and all diplomats spoke mostly that. Because Mother had gone to a French convent school her French was "très élégant," and so she had the time of her life. She was also a great flirt, which I watched from afar.

With all of these good times, even Mother got exhausted and decided she must have some rest. So, for two months of the year, we drove in a horse-drawn wagon to a Buddhist temple in the Western Hills quite a distance outside Peking. This lovely place was called the Temple of One Hundred Courtyards. We occupied five or six courtyards. The monks remained in the others, and I grew to know the courtyards and the monks very well.

Because Father had told me I could have whatever pet I wanted if I learned Chinese, I learned the language quickly, thereby acquiring a pony, a donkey, five hedgehogs, and three dogs. I had long conversations with the household staff (we had a houseful, as in those days the dollar was riding the economic waves). Speaking Chinese has had an enormous influence on my life and having much time to myself, particularly at the temple, I became quite a talker and spent hour after hour with the priests. They told me that everything in nature was as much alive as I was. Every tree and every flower must be respected and you must let them know that you know that they—and particularly a venerable tree—must be given real love, a touch, and a happy word—these will prolong their lives and enhance yours.

"What about a wooden chair?" I asked anxiously. "After all, it was a tree once. Is it all right to sit on it?" "Of course it is all right to sit on it," they answered. "It is doing the work which it was intended to do after its happy life in this world. Everyone and everything must do its service so as to worship Buddha in the world to come." Although my idea of Buddha was very vague (I only knew him as a rather inscrutable statue), still I loved my long chats. The monks were very indulgent with me, and of course their kindness and good manners made a great impression on me. All my life since then, nature has meant so much to me. If I feel depressed or in a bad humor, or worried, the mood will not last long if I am walking in the magnificent woods of Maine or watching the sunset on the Hudson River.

When we returned to America after four unforgettable years in China, Father was ordered to Washington. I loved it there because I had adoring grandparents who opened up another world to me, particularly my maternal grandfather, who was English and read Shakespeare to me and played cockney songs on his candle-lit piano. But even more important than the fun I had in their house (we had our own house, which belonged to my father's family) was the interest that my father took in the opening of my religious horizon. One day, Father said, "Brooke must go to church," a sentiment I had never heard before. As far as I was concerned, a church did not exist except as a place to do sightseeing in Paris or London. Father now having returned to Washington, he remembered his own childhood and his father's having been on the vestry of St. John's Episcopal Church, across Lafayette Square from the White House. Miraculously, a perfect person came into my life—an elderly spinster called Miss Elsa Bancroft Bliss, a relative of Father's and also a close relative of George Bancroft, the historian. To me she became Aunt Elsa, a woman of strong religious principles and one who, as I look back, must have felt that in being close to me and in teaching me (a little heathen in her eyes) the word of God, she was doing her duty and one which she enjoyed. She was totally devoid of a sense of humor or of a light touch of any kind. On the other hand, I think she got real pleasure bringing me into the church, and as for me, I loved it. I felt in many of the prayers and hymns a kinship to my priests in China. The Lord's Prayer and the beautiful day prayers "for the means of grace and the hope of glory" inspired the same wonderful remoteness yet closeness that I had felt in the temples and feel now when I walk through the forests.

There is, however, something more in Christianity that appealed to my nature most of all and that was its teaching to care for and be interested in other people. If Buddha is remote from the real world, that is not for me. I am interested in all people, all types, all colors. To have been left a foundation to work with, which has enabled me to enhance the cultural and physical life of New York City, has been the greatest gift that could have been given to me.

PATCHWORK CHILD

Chapter 1

Introduction
to the
Patchwork

Although I am a child of the twentieth century, my background and childhood are so foreign to the life of today that in describing them I seem to be stealing pages from a nineteenth-century novelist, or at least an Edwardian memoir. I have friends the same age as I whose life in childhood was very similar to the life of a child of the present time. But it was not so with me. I was removed, by circumstances and the character of my family, from the ordinary current of life. To isolate me even more was the fact that I was an only child and it seemed that everything depended on my being able to come to terms with the Grown-up world. The Grown-ups in my life were positive and intense, and their likes and dislikes, fads and fancies, filtered down to me and colored my whole existence. In order to have a secret life of my own (which was very important to me) I learned at an early age, in fact before I was even conscious of it, to play the part that was expected of me. I tried to be a good child because it was so much easier to be good than to have the Grown-ups cross. When Mother said, "Do as I say, *not* as I do," *I* took it as a very proper sentiment coming from a Grown-up. I simply stored away in my mind the things Mother or her friends did and bided the time when I would be a Grown-up lady and mistress of all I surveyed. But in the meantime I tried to create a crude little light of my own in the midst of the blinding radiance that was Mother.

Because of my father's military profession we moved from place to place and I had to adjust myself not only to the Grown-ups but also to new schools, new friends, a new way of life. It made me shy and insecure and it became terribly important to me to have friends. But it also taught me that in order to have friends one must put oneself out for them and take nothing for granted. This is not a bad thing to learn and so, although I learned little in the ordinary way of schooling in my peripatetic and Jane Austen–like childhood, still I did pick up a few useful things to support me in later life.

I did not, of course, like Athena, spring full-panoplied from

(previous page)
Me on my first day out in Peking after having been ill from a reaction to a typhoid injection

the brow of Zeus. Like everyone else, I am blood and bone and characteristics of my forebears. Father and Mother were the Twin Beacons guiding me through babyhood and the crepuscule of childhood to adolescence. As I grew older I came to realize that they were also John and Mabel. I loved them both in entirely different ways because they *were* so different. What made them dissimilar was not necessarily their backgrounds (both had ancestors buried in the best and oldest graveyards in the country). But they were really fire and water or perhaps, as I learned in China, "the yang and the yin," the male and the female principles of life. Father was all male, Mother all female—a very fine combination.*

Father, as the son of an admiral, was brought up in the tradition of the Service and naturally wanted to go to Annapolis. My grandfather, however, was very much against it. Grandfather felt that the Navy was getting too big, that it was no longer "a gentleman's profession," and that there was little chance "to make a mark." Grandfather Russell hated the thought of "being in trade," but he was more broad-minded and wanted Father to branch out. He refused to lift a finger to get Father appointed to Annapolis and would not even discuss the matter. My father, however, was determined to have his way. As the family was living in Washington, Father had an advantage—he knew that the President had the power to appoint a certain number of candidates to the Naval Academy. So he, at the age of fifteen, boldly went to the White House and asked to see the President. It seems extraordinary to me today but President Cleveland *did* see him and Father explained what he wanted. The President was hesitant at first and told Father that his last appointees had not been very successful; he was not sure that he wanted to appoint any more.

"You can be sure, Mr. President," said Father, "that I will succeed. You can put your trust in me." (Arthur Krock of *The New York Times* told this story in the *Times* after Father's death.)

*See note about my family background at end of book.

Here I am at about nine months old, all dressed up and ready to go to Dupont Circle

The President laughed and Father went home. A few days later a letter arrived saying that Father had been appointed. My grandfather was so delighted by Father's initiative and determination that he gave his consent and there was rejoicing in the family.

Father did what he told the President he would do. He became a brilliant officer—with imagination and dash. He became major general commandant of the Marine Corps and was for eight years (under Harding and Hoover) high commissioner to Haiti with the rank of ambassador. As high commissioner he had to cast aside his military role and apply himself tactfully to the reorganizing of a country which had descended into chaos. That he did so successfully is shown in this quotation from a letter from President Hoover:

> The material progress which has been achieved during the eight years of your incumbency of the office of High Commissioner is substantial and impressive. Haitian finances have been placed on a sound basis, commerce has revived, adequate roads now connect the important cities, schools and hospitals have been built, agriculture and industries have been developed and encouraged and outstanding work has been accomplished in introducing sanitary measures through the entire Republic. These results have been largely due to your administrative ability and the high-minded purpose which has animated you in the performance of your task.

But I am rushing ahead. Father was only a young Marine captain on a spring evening in the early 1900s when, dressed in his full-dress uniform, he went to a ball. The full-dress uniform was a beautiful thing—the gold-encrusted monkey jacket, the light-blue trousers with the red stripe, the white gloves and gold epaulets. He had coal-black hair, dark eyes, and a trim figure and, though not a dedicated dancer, he was an excellent waltzer. All in all, an attractive young man in his late twenties. As "The Blue Danube" was struck up he was introduced to a Miss Howard and asked her to dance. She accepted demurely and off they went spinning over the floor, not realizing that they were waltzing into forty-seven years of married life.

Father took a good look at the girl in his arms. She had nat-

As "The Blue Danube" was struck up, Father was introduced to a Miss Howard and asked her to dance. She accepted demurely and off they went spinning over the floor, not realizing that they were waltzing into forty-seven years of married life.

urally curly dark hair piled on top of her head, sparkling brown eyes, a merry mouth, and a pretty figure. She was in her early twenties and was dressed in white tulle with blue satin bows. When the music stopped they had a glass of punch and Father asked permission to call. They had never met before but the families had known each other so there was a bond in common. (My father was an orphan by that time.)

When Mother told her family the next day that Father had asked permission to call, Granny snorted. "A Marine officer!" she said. "A Sea Urchin! I certainly don't want to encourage a penniless creature like that with no prospects."

Grandfather immediately took the opposite side. "Mabel will not see him alone, Bertie," he said, "her sisters will be with her. He may have no prospects but he is a gentleman and will know how to conduct himself. I see no harm in letting him come." Granny tossed her head. "Mark my word, Mr. Howard," she said, "if you leave the latch up for every penniless young man, it will all end in a pretty kettle of fish."

She was right, the latch was indeed up, and Father, although calm in the drawing room, was very bold when alone with Mother. They sneaked off for a walk in Rock Creek Park and in a secluded spot he put his arms about her and kissed her. "You are the girl I am going to marry," he said. "You must ask Papa [pronounced pa*pa*] first," she murmured. "I will tomorrow," he said firmly. "Now just give me another kiss."

Mother, of course, could not wait for tomorrow. When she got home she rushed to tell her sisters, who were sitting in the Morning Room. "You're a fool," said her eldest sister, Clare. "What's so wonderful about him? I wouldn't look at him twice." "You're jealous because you're getting to be an old maid," snapped Mother. Aunt Clare gave Mother a good hearty slap in the face. "I've turned down ten men better than John Russell," she cried. Mother gave Aunt Clare a good slap back. "No, you haven't!" she shrieked. "Only that horrible old man from New York that no one wanted."

Grandfather Howard dressed in his summer outfit

Mother and me outside my grandparents' house

My Howard grandparents at Greystone, their house in the Green Spring Valley, Maryland

Their voices rose higher and higher. Grandfather called down from his workshop above (he had a passion for cabinetmaking and for working on old clocks). "Girls, girls, stop that infernal racket. Can't a man have a little peace in his own house?"

Mother ran out into the hall and called up the stairs. She knew that she was Grandfather's favorite. "Papa," she moaned, "Clare slapped me." "And *why* did she do that?" inquired Grandfather, looking over the banister. "Because I want to marry John Russell," said Mother, still sobbing.

Grandfather descended the stairs. "What's that you're saying?" he demanded. "Marry, marry, what is this talk of marrying?"

Mother clung to Grandfather. "Oh, I do want to marry him, Papa," she pleaded. "I love him so much."

In spite of this stormy start, which was typical of the Howard household, where high spirits and high tempers ran hand in hand, everything calmed down and eventually the entire family was won over to Father. He not only had a little money of his own, but also owned a small house in Washington on the corner of De Sales and Seventeenth streets. It was a cream-colored brick house with a New Orleans–type grilled porch, a little garden with flowering bushes, and a brick garden path which ended at a little iron gate. Father promised Grandfather that he would always keep it so that Mother would have a home. In other words, he was not really a Sea Urchin, but an amphibious animal. Surrounded by a beaming family, Father and Mother were married in June by Bishop Harding in the drawing room of the Howard house on N Street.

This book, however, is about me, not about them. I caught up with them very quickly, as I was born the following March. From then on I was an "on-the-spot reporter," "an interested observer," or whatever you wish to call it, until my marriage sixteen years later. Little pitchers do indeed have big ears, and when they start keeping diaries, as I did at seven, all is garbled grist to their mills.

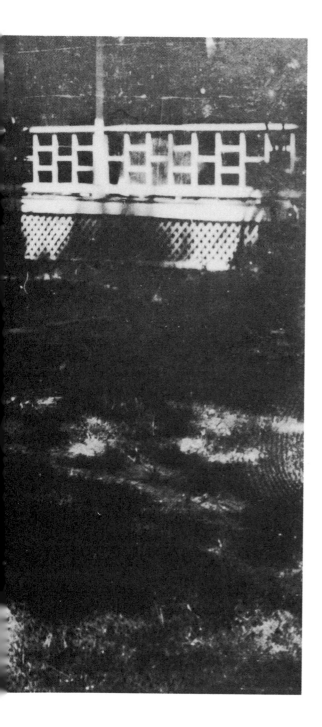

Chapter 2

Howards
and Marines
and First Duty
in Hawaii

Father and Mother lived happily in Portsmouth, New Hampshire, from the time they were married until I was three months old. Then Father was ordered on a tour of sea duty to the Orient which was to last three years. Mother and I went back to live with my grandparents on N Street. In spite of all their rows and tensions, the Howards had "family feeling" and they rallied round "poor Mabel." Mother found it a little hard to take some of the digs that her sister Clare gave—some of the "I told you so" type of thing. But aside from that, no serious ruptures took place because there was always me to fall back on. I made a great diversion in their lives. There were seven Howards in all and they practically tore me apart passing me from one to the other. Even Granny, seeing Mother bathing me one day and letting my head slip, grabbed me dripping from the little rubber tub and carried me off to her room, declaring that Mother was "not fit to have a child." According to the family tales, never had a baby received so much love. When Lena, the nurse, had her day off, they all, including my young uncle Charlie, fought for the privilege of pushing my pram up to Dupont Circle. Twice a day Grandfather's old Irish terrier, Patsy, considered it his duty to march solemnly beside the pram. When it came time for him to go to dog heaven, he trotted off by himself to Dupont Circle and lay down to die under the bench where my nurse used to sit. It was considered a great tribute to me that Patsy should be faithful even unto death.

So I started forth rather royally, surrounded by adoration and homage. Mother was nothing loath to have me the center of attention. After all, she was the only Howard daughter with a baby. The battle of the adults for my person, and for my emerging intelligence, sharpened my perception and I think that my memory starts earlier than most. Who can say whether it is really what I remember or what I have been told over and over again? I do not pretend to know. I can only say that from about age two and a half, I remember things as they appeared to me, not necessarily accurately but like

(previous page)
Near our house in Honolulu

huge vague shadows in my mind or like splendid sparkling episodes.

My first memory is of communication, which, I suppose, set the habit for the long telephone talks I have enjoyed with my friends all through my life, much to the fury of my three husbands (the only thing they had in common).

Granny's house possessed two mysterious forms of communication—one used by everyone, the other used only by me. The one common to the entire household was the speaking tube. It was a hole with a little brass cover on the wall at the height of a Grown-up's mouth. One pulled up the brass flap and called down it. It communicated with the basement kitchen and pantry and, when one called, a weird, whistling sound came back. Aunt Nancy, an ex-slave who was cook, or Melissa, the waitress, would answer and their voices, sounding eerie and strange, would float up from the nether regions. "Yes, ma'am" would reach the ear like the cry of a dying banshee. I used to be lifted up to call down the tube, and when I got an answer I would put my hands over my ears and shudder from a delicious, but secure, terror.

The other communication was the heating system. The house was heated by hot air, which came up through covered gratings on the floor. Mother read *The Jungle Book* to me about this time and I got the idea that a beast called Mowgli Frog lived down there. I used to sit on the floor and, leaning over the grating, would call to Mowgli Frog to answer me. Sometimes he did, which was when my young uncle was at home and howled back at me from the cellar. But if I listened and listened and there was no response, I would scramble up and walk away, saying stoically, "Nenna mind."

Every night I went through the ritual of kissing Father's picture. It was made almost into an icon, with flowers in front of it and little things he sent me around it. In the picture he was in his uniform as a midshipman and beneath the picture was a snapshot of the ship that he was on then. I kissed his picture and

The battle of the adults for my person, and for my emerging intelligence, sharpened my perception and I think that my memory starts earlier than for most people . . . from about age two and a half, I remember things as they appeared to me, not necessarily accurately but like huge vague shadows in my mind, or like splendid sparkling episodes.

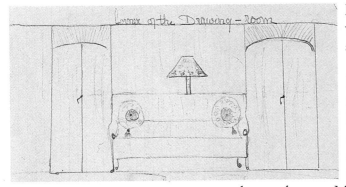
The drawing room

learned to say, "Father on the Big Ship," while relatives and friends watched amusedly.

When the great day arrived and Father returned, I was not as bright as I might have been. Lena dressed me and brought me down all starched out in an embroidered dress with a low-slung sash around my fat little body. I saw them all, the entire family and a few friends, clustered around a man. Mother was hanging on his arm and laughing and, for the first time, no one seemed aware of me. I clung to Lena's hand and looked up into her face. "Lena," I said, "who's that man?" Lena laughed. "Why, that's Father off the Big Ship," she said. With that I gave a yell of joy and, running through the crowd, threw myself against his knees. He lifted me up in his arms and we looked each other in the eye. "Why, it's a Little Woman," he said, laughing. He gave me a big hug and I clung to him. From then until the day of his death "Little Woman" was his nickname for me.

Things were different now that Father was at home. Almost at once we went on to Annapolis, where Father taught at the Naval Academy for a year. We had a nice little house in one of those long, monotonous rows that always have existed and apparently always will exist on government posts. Our very own things appeared, objects strange and new on tables and mantelpieces. They were wedding presents that had been packed away and were now brought out. I saw for the first time ornaments that were to follow us from pillar to post, some of them surviving so that they are still about today, others chipped, broken, discarded, and lost during our various moves. My grandparents' house on N Street was dark and full of leather-bound books, charcoal rubbings of English tombs, and steel engravings of scenes from Shakespeare. This little house by contrast was all light and sunshine and prettiness. To me the most beautiful thing was a round crystal clock with a magnifying glass over its face so that the numerals seemed enormous; there were huge rhinestones all around it which made it sparkle and glitter when the sun struck it, and I used to stand entranced in front of it. Mother had started to read fairy stories to me and I thought it was a Fairy Clock. When I asked, I was told that it was indeed a Fairy Clock and from then on I used to rush into the room unexpectedly, hoping to catch a glimpse of the fairies who had made it and came to wind it every day.

It was in Annapolis that I first saw Marines. In those days every officer had a house orderly to look after the government property, which meant keeping the furnace stoked, cutting the grass, and occasionally turning the ice-cream freezer handle. There was one orderly who was forever teasing me. "Hello, little boy," he would say day after day and I, panting with indignation, would answer, "I'm not a boy, I'm a girl!" One day, though, he made me specially mad and in a fury I yelled out, "I'm a girl! And you, you are a"—I searched for something terrible and came out with—"you . . . are an old ginger-ale bottle!"

Mother overheard this from upstairs and she and Lena rushed out. I smiled to welcome them but it was not my side they took. "You are a naughty girl," exclaimed Mother. "You are not a little lady," said Lena. I was taken aback. I knew that not to be a little lady was a dreadful thing and I already wanted to be one. I wanted to sing and play the piano like Mother and Tantee (my youngest aunt, who was staying with us) and to have a Fairy Clock of my own. This was my idea of being a lady and, at the age of three, that was my goal.

I saw a great many Marines during my childhood but the Marines I knew from then on never teased me. They were my friends and often my playmates in the years to come, and I took it for granted that we should like one another. I was proud of them, a race of men apart, defenders of their country, and of unqualified courage and daring. When I read about King Arthur I felt quite at home. These were simply Marines in another costume.

My grandparents' house on N Street was dark and full of leather-bound books, charcoal rubbings of English tombs, and steel engravings of scenes from Shakespeare.

Hardly had I become used to the house in Annapolis, with its wedding presents displayed and its cozy boxlike rooms, when we were ordered away. The Marines came and packed the ornaments and china into barrels, and the place was soon a stark, semiempty shell of a house with bits of excelsior blowing across the floors. We lingered on in this atmosphere midst floods of tears from my mother and aunts and grandmother and Lena. Grandfather and Uncle Charlie remained stoical, but Father went around whistling and singing little tunes. He longed to have Mother really to himself and to show her the world. Dear Lena was being left behind, the first of many sad partings for me. She had been the person closest to me since I became conscious of other human beings and I could not imagine life without her. At the train my sobs were so prolonged that they became mingled with hiccups and I grew red in the face. The family rushed me into the dining car and immediately ordered vanilla ice cream for me. When it came I pushed the plate away. I did not want ice cream. I wanted Lena.

"Eat your ice cream. It will make you feel better," urged Mother. I shook my head and stifled a sob. Father smiled at me. "You don't know what's good," he said. "I want Lena," I whispered. "Oh, but think how wonderful to be in a train eating ice cream on your way to Honolulu." Father bent over and, picking up the spoon, popped some ice cream into my mouth. It was good. I swallowed it. "And now," said Father, patting my hand, "you are a big girl." "Why am I a big girl?" I demanded. "Because you know what's good!" he said, laughing. It did not make up for the loss of Lena but it helped to be told that one was a "big girl."

Mother was longing to branch out. Those three years at home with the family had been pretty tedious. But "Après la pluie comes le beau temps," as they said in the convent, and how true it was. Honolulu was marvelous. We settled in a cottage right near the beach of Waikiki with a wonderful view of famous Diamond Head, everything more beautiful than she had ever dreamed of. There was no seawall in those days and the Pacific rolled almost up to the lovely green grass. The lushness of it all was intoxicating. The abundance of flowers, the delicate scent of the tuberoses, the graceful palm trees—life in the Marine Corps was not bad at all. In fact, it was paradise, as Mother wrote home to her sisters.

Mother was still in her twenties and Father in his early thirties. She began to discover what a talent she had for enjoying herself, and Father had the vitality to keep up with her. He was pleased that she enjoyed their first "duty" together, and she, who had never traveled except on Grandfather's magic carpet of books, found every new experience fascinating. There were luaus, or picnics, typically Island music, and there were dances and bridge parties and excursions to the other islands. The days were all cloudless and the nights star-spangled.

For me it was a different story. Gone was the security of N Street and Annapolis and Lena. Gone the comforting familiarity of the pattern of my life and the hand of Lena clasped in mine. For me it was the place where I first knew fear—not just ordinary fear but the fear that comes at night and paralyzes one's will, the fear of the unknown and unrecognizable. I had a Japanese nurse, Olo San, a pretty, apparently gay creature who to this day my mother still insists was one of the best nurses I ever had. What Mother never knew, because I was too young to tell her, was that Olo San was a prey to ageless superstition.

There was a house that we passed every day on our way to the beach. It stood hidden behind a high salmon-pink hibiscus hedge. Here something fearful had happened: according to Olo San, a man had hanged himself up like an old stocking from the ceiling, his eyes had popped out and so had his tongue, and his face had grown a dreadful purple. This had made the man extremely unhappy and he was never able to leave the house. He was there, night and day. When we passed his house, Olo San ran and my fat little legs could hardly keep up with her because it seemed that this horrid man was lonely and wanted someone

In Waikiki trying to make a lei with my Japanese nurse, who terrified me (at right)

to keep him company. When one of the hibiscus flowers brushed my face, I almost screamed because I felt it was his hand reaching for me. Once safely beyond the house, I forgot him and played happily on the beach, building castles and digging moats. Though only three and a half at the time, I remember the beauty of that blue, blue water and shining beach.

At night, though, the fears came back. Olo San, who I suppose wanted some time to herself, told me that I must go to sleep at once or the devils would get me. I used to try awfully hard, but sleep did not always come and then I would hear the devils laughing and shouting. I know now that they were simply Grown-ups having a very good time, particularly as the noise was worse on moonlit nights. But not knowing this then, I would pull the covers over my head and hold on to an old flannel rag that I loved.

Father and Mother adored Honolulu, but Waikiki became too gay even for them, and so they took a house up in the mountains. I was much happier there. There was no man with a purple tongue or devils dancing at night. And, better still, Father and Mother were at home with me at night.

I remember the house vaguely. What I liked was that it was built on the side of a hill and one came in on the drawing-room floor and went downstairs to the bedroom. We had just unpacked and everything was put into its proper place when Father got his orders—and such dreadful orders! Mother burst into tears. . . . Panama! An outlandish, strange place where someone called Goethals was digging a canal.

Chapter 3

Panama: Red Dust,
Mosquitoes, and Roses
(and a Mad Dog)

The contrast between Honolulu and Panama was enormous. Whereas all was lush and green and fresh in Honolulu, in Panama there was nothing but red earth, red dust, and a broiling, barren wasteland. We lived in a camp overhanging one of the large "cuts" that were being built to make the Canal. The little wooden bungalows of the camp stood forlornly in a row along a cinder path, which was artistically outlined in true Marine fashion by a border of whitewashed stones. To add to the wretchedness of the place, the noise was indescribable. All day long the motley gangs of laborers working on the Canal were shouting, cursing, yelling, or singing in every known language, and this incessant roar was punctuated by dynamite blasts. From dawn to dusk this racket went on, and when the sun set, great swarms of mosquitoes rose up and filled the air. To Mother it was a real inferno and she spent the first weeks weeping and listlessly trying to teach me to read.

Then came a break in this dreary monotony. Father and Mother went into Panama City to dine at the legation with the American minister, Mr. Squires, his wife, and their daughters, Helen and Gladys. The Squireses were charming, well-bred, cultivated people who lived in a civilized way. There were silver candlesticks with pink shades on the polished table, servants in white gloves quietly and efficiently passing the food, and a French chef in the kitchen. It was like coming upon an oasis, Mother always said, after being lost in the desert. At this dinner party three things happened—two important, one funny.

The funny thing concerned the aforementioned French chef, who was a master at making spun sugar. The dessert arrived, a great Siamese-like tower of ice cream and whipped cream rising from a huge bed of spun sugar. The dessert course was served with finger bowls on the dessert plate, each with a little lace doily between finger bowl and plate. The French minister took off the finger bowl but not the doily, and Mother and Mrs. Squires looked up in horror when, as he was complimenting Mrs. Squires on the excellent "entremets," they saw hanging with a

(previous page)
On my pony near the Panama Canal. On the right is the turned-up dirt from the digging of the Canal.

bit of spun sugar from his mouth a tiny end of Mrs. Squires's best Brussels lace. He gave a gulp of appreciation and it was gone—too late to pull it out or caution him. This incident was a great bond between Mrs. Squires and Mother, and apparently had no ill effect at all on Monsieur le Ministre.

More important, at this dinner Mother met two people who were to do a great deal for her—one, materially; the other, mentally. The first was Colonel (later General) Goethals, the engineer of the Canal, a strikingly handsome white-haired man who took an immediate fancy to Father and Mother and listened sympathetically to Mother's tale of the horror of our camp. The next day he sent out his carpenters to build a vast, screened veranda embellished with hanging pots of orchids and ferns and begonias and huge tubs of oleanders and hibiscus. Outside he built a rose garden. He came often to see that all these plants were being well cared for, and I grew very fond of his gentle pat on the top of my head. The other person had a much more lasting effect on Mother (and, incidentally, on me). His name was Henry May and he was a raffiné, sophisticated, cultivated young man serving as secretary of the legation. He was a gentleman to his fingertips, incapable of being unkind or rude, and educated in both the heart and the mind.

Years later I saw Henry May in Venice, when on an October afternoon he took me to see the Tintorettos at the Scuola di San Rocco. The light was poor and dear Henry was almost blind, but he led me eagerly up to a certain corner, anxious that I should get the most out of the paintings. "Look from here, Brooke," he said enthusiastically; "from here one really gets the best idea of the beauty and the grace." I stood with him in the corner, looking sadly at the picture as Henry continued talking, urging me to notice this and that exquisite detail. It was so dark that I could see nothing, but he who was blind saw everything. It was all stored away in the treasure house of his mind. Such a man was Henry May, and the influence he had on my mother during those months in Panama was great. He was more than a

All day long the motley gangs of laborers working on the Canal were shouting, cursing, yelling, or singing in every known language, and this incessant roar was punctuated by dynamite blasts. From dawn to dusk this racket went on, and when the sun set, great swarms of mosquitoes rose up and filled the air.

resource, he was a signpost to a new way of life. Without him Mother would never have got out of Peking what she did.

I had no Lena in Panama but, thank heaven, no Olo San either! We had a bedraggled old woman who was supposed to do everything for us, and Mother thought that she could "make do" in this primitive place with this literally skeleton staff, but it was really too much for her. Mother had decided to take full charge of me, with the best intentions, but my horizon at five was necessarily limited and I became a bit of a bore after I had gone through all my tricks. She said that she simply must have someone to press her clothes and help with me. Such a person did not seem to exist and the other Marine officers' wives lifted their eyebrows in disapproval. Most of them had no one at all. It began to worry Father that Mother was making a slave of herself, ruining her hands and skin in this hellspot, turning herself into a boring "Service wife" with no time to read Dr. Eliot's "five-foot shelf," which she had brought with her. He wanted Mother to remain pretty and attractive and, above all, happy, so he volunteered to solve the problem.

"I will get someone when I go into Panama City tomorrow," he said. "I will find someone for you and Little Woman." "How can you possibly?" demanded Mother. "A properly trained maid doesn't exist here." "I'll find one," said Father firmly, "and will bring her home with me." Mother laughed rather skeptically. But that is just what he did!

He was walking along the street in Panama City when in front of him a young woman came out of the patio of the President's Palace. She was a pretty, golden-skinned mulatto with neatly parted black hair, a black silk dress, and little red velvet slippers. She looked meekly at Father as he passed her and he suddenly became emboldened to speak to her.

"Por favor," he began, then lapsing into English, "I am looking for a maid to wait on a lady and a little girl . . . perhaps you would know of such a person." "Yes, sir," she said, speaking English with an attractive foreign accent. "I am looking for just such a position. I am French, from Guadeloupe, and I thought there was a place chez Monsieur le Président but it has already been filled. If you wish a reference, come with me to the consulate of Guadeloupe."

Father went with her, found her reference perfect, and brought her home in triumph that very evening. Her name was Clarisse and she stayed with us until we left, always wearing her little red slippers. She taught me French nursery rhymes and I liked her, but I was beginning to have my own interests.

The rose garden that General Goethals had given us was my favorite spot. I have no idea how large it was, but to me it seemed a veritable forest of roses. I used to crawl under the rosebushes until I got into the very middle of the bed, and there I would sit in the sweet-smelling shade watching the busy insect life around me. The insects liked me, too, as I was round, pink, and soft, and soon my legs and arms were encased in wrappings of bandages, and the scent of roses was drowned out by the smell of citronella on my face.

I would not give up this lovely place, though, even if I had to suffer for it. I shall never again see roses so enormous or foliage so green. I liked the warm, earthy smell and the scent of the roses and the fact that it was practically an impregnable fortress. No one else knew just how to creep in or would dare face all those huge thorns.

From this retreat I emerged one day to have some fruit juice. Mother was sitting on the veranda talking to Henry May. They were laughing and I gathered Mother was telling a story about Mrs. X (the wife of a fellow officer). "Her house," said Mother, "shows her up . . . it looks just like a summer boardinghouse."

I finished my drink and, as I listened, my curiosity was aroused. What was a summer boardinghouse? What was special about it that made it so funny? *I* wanted to laugh, too. Mrs. X's house was only one away from ours and I decided to go over and have a look. I slipped away unobserved and followed the cinder path outlined by whitewashed stones that went past the officers'

. . . Colonel (later General) Goethals, the engineer of the Canal, a strikingly handsome white-haired man. . . took an immediate fancy to Father and Mother and listened sympathetically to Mother's tale of the horror of our camp. The next day he sent out his carpenters to build a vast, screened veranda embellished with hanging pots of orchids and ferns and begonias and huge tubs of oleanders and hibiscus. Outside he built a rose garden.

quarters. When I got to Mrs. X's, I stood in the middle of the path and started solemnly to inspect the house. Except that it didn't have the Goethals veranda, it looked very much like our house. It had a porch in front with a long row of rocking chairs, which I thought was very nice.

I was standing there quietly looking it over when Mrs. X opened the screen door and came out onto the porch. "Hello, Brooke," she said gaily, "what are you doing here?" "I came to look at your house," I said, dropping a curtsy. "To look at my house!" she exclaimed. "Why, what's the matter with it?" "Well, it's making Mother laugh," I said, looking up at her. "She says it's just like a summer boardinghouse."

Mrs. X's face underwent a horrid change. "She says that, does she?" she snapped. "The stuck-up snob, I'll tell her a thing or two!" and ran back into the house.

I sighed. What made one Grown-up laugh seemed to make another one cross. It would be nice to go home where the fun was.

But when I got home Mr. May had gone, and so had the fun. Mother was waiting for me on the steps. "You wretched child," she said, as I drew near. "What have you done? What have you told Mrs. X? She was so wild on the telephone I couldn't make out what she was saying."

I repeated dully what I had said and Mother burst into tears. "Go to your room and stay there," she said, "you really deserve a good spanking." She started toward me with her hand upraised. I ran as fast as my legs could carry me and scrambled under my bed, which was conveniently placed against a wall. Mother got down on her hands and knees and tried to reach me, but I made myself into a round ball, totally inaccessible. Mother finally gave up and went back to the veranda. I knew that I would be safe until Father got home. It gave me time to ruminate on the fact that Grown-ups were a strange and alien race, undependable and erratic. I never again told one of them what another one said (at least not until I was grown up myself).

This same Mrs. X was involved in another incident. She and her husband and the couple living next to them kept chickens in order to have fresh eggs. These chickens were of the same breed and, being carefree and gregarious, wandered back and forth between the two backyards. This caused a certain amount of acrimony between the two couples. Finally, after several disputes, Captain X painted a green stripe on his chickens and Lieutenant Y put a red stripe on his. All went well for a week. But the Marines heard of this and one fine morning the X's and the Y's woke up to find all the chickens with both a red and a green stripe on them, and utter confusion reigned!

I learned of this on the day when Father called the Marines together and gave them a talk, threatening dire punishment if such pranks continued. Our orderly was there, and as I had seen him hiding some red and green paint the night before, I knew that he had had a hand in it. However, true to my new philosophy, I preferred not to get mixed up in the Grown-up world.

Father was not with us all the time. Once a month he went on an inspection trip to distant camps and was gone for a week or ten days. There was one camp so unattractive that it was called Camp Diablo. It was while he was there that Father was bitten by a mad dog. He was in his dressing gown and bedroom slippers on his way to the shower when the dog came up and took a nip of his heel. Father loved dogs, and he laughed. But the dog ran through the camp biting thirteen of the men so that they had to shoot him down. When the doctor examined the dog's head he found it seething with rabies. The men and Father were rushed back to our camp and the doctor came and told us that we must leave at once because the Pasteur treatment had to be started within fourteen days or the men would go mad.

It was in the days before airplanes but, fortunately, there was a transport sailing from Colón which would get us back to Washington in time. Father looked pale and shaken, but Mother, in spite of her anxiety, was pleased to be leaving. She sang as she superintended the packing of the boxes and danced by herself on the empty veranda. I was glad to be going, too. And even when I sat in the rose garden for the last time I was not sad. I had no dog, no friends, my mosquito bites itched dreadfully, and it was July and very hot. There was little to beguile the eye or stimulate the mind at that broiling camp perched on the scorched earth overlooking the muddy water.

The trip home was unbearably hot, too. The ship plowed through a molten sea, and every evening the sun sank below the horizon, a round red ball. There was such tension among the Grown-ups aboard that even I felt it.

One day the meaning of this tension was brought home to me. I was peering through the rail, looking down on the afterdeck where some Marines were playing shuffleboard, when suddenly a man on all fours ran through the doorway. He raced along the deck, shaking his head and howling. The shuffleboard players tried to catch him, but he eluded them and, with a last, ear-piercing howl, jumped overboard. "Man overboard!" someone yelled, and immediately a grinding noise came from the engine room as the ship began to slow down.

I watched the man until he sank, and then ran as fast as I could to the bow of the ship, where Father and Mother were stretched out in their deck chairs trying to catch a breeze. Mother was reading but Father was looking listlessly out to sea. I climbed onto Father's chair. "Father," I cried, "I just saw a man running like a dog and then he jumped overboard." I nuzzled my face against Father's neck.

Father's neck was cold and clammy and, for the only time in my life, I felt him trembling. "There, there, Little Woman," he said comfortingly, "don't worry, they will find him." "Oh, God," said Mother, and reached over to take Father's hand. Father gave me a hug and smiled at her. "Don't you worry either, Mabs," he said. "We have only two days more and I rather expected this. That man was a poor specimen anyway . . . he should never have been in the Marine Corps."

I knew Marines were the bravest people in the world and if this man was not a real Marine I did not feel so bad.

In spite of our anxiety, we reached home safely. The Pasteur treatment was terrible and one man, refusing to continue after twelve injections, also went mad. But Father bore the treatment with real stoicism, and we had Grandfather with us to keep our spirits up.

All's well that ends well. The mad dog really did us a good turn. We got away from Panama, had a happy time with Grandfather, then went to Maine for a lovely vacation in the pinewoods.

Chapter 4

"If the Day
It Had
Been Finer . . ."

After Panama we went to Newport, where Father was to teach at the War College. We had a little house on Bellevue Avenue, next to the Reading Room. The house was painted dark green and had a garden with a small coach house at the bottom of it, which made a good and rather mysterious place to play. I had an inefficient young Irish nurse, called Jenny, and a Boston bulldog called Silverking. Silverking was somewhat unsuccessful. He was one of those timid, quivering dogs with no personality. I tried to like him because Father had given him to me, but even Father, who was always throwing bones for him and trying to get him to play, found it uphill work and eventually we gave him to a bachelor officer who seemed to love him. I think Silverking did not like his name, or children, because the bachelor called him Tom and he was quite happy there.

It was in Newport that I was introduced to the "children's party." Up to that time I had not played with any children, and the transition from the solitude of Panama to a community of children who all knew one another and were experts at pinning the tail on the donkey or jumping into a chair at "musical chairs" was more than I could cope with. I simply stood and watched them and wished that I was safe back in the rose garden in Panama. I dreaded climbing another flight of steps flanked with great tubs of blue hydrangeas, to be greeted on the porch by smiling mothers and a row of little girls and boys. I preferred to climb a copper beech tree and hang along a branch.

These parties, however, often had redeeming features. There was a delightful game, called "spiderweb," where one was given the end of a piece of string and followed it on its tortuous course under chairs and sofas and behind pictures until one came upon a lovely present, maybe a little purse or a Brownie camera. Once I got a glass bowl with two goldfish in it. I called them Katie and Harry and developed a pleasant habit of sticking a toe into the bowl and letting them nibble on it. I grew so fond of them that I had them always on the table by my bed. Unfortunately, the table was also near the window and I woke up one winter morning to find them frozen stiff, their eyes turned toward me. I insisted on thawing them out, but it was of no avail and I had to bury them together in a little box down at the bottom of the garden. I never wanted fish again because Katie and Harry looked so piteous in their ice water.

It was in this bedroom, as I lay in bed one morning watching the sunlight on the wall, that I suddenly realized that if you put "b" before "room" you had the word "broom." I was six at the time and it seemed a magnificent revelation. From then on I was busy learning words and a whole new world opened for me. I began to write and discovered that what I had in my mind could be put on paper. *That* was exciting, too. Mother always said that Miss Sayre's was just a little "dame's" school (not to be confused with the current slang) but I think it must have been better than that to have inspired me so.

It was in Newport that I started telling myself continued stories. After I was put to bed and the lights were turned out and the Grown-ups had gone away, I would start where I had left off the night before. It was a great comfort, as I was afraid of the dark and telling myself a story was like having another person with me. Sometimes, though, I would get tremendously excited—stories seemed to unfold without any guidance on my part—and my thoughts would come so fast that I would have to sit up in bed to calm down. Then I would begin to get frightened and suddenly realize that I was alone. I would get out of bed and, in my bare feet, tiptoe down the hall to see where the Grown-ups were, as I longed for the reassurance of another voice. Mother and Father went out a great deal and sometimes Jenny, who was supposed to stay with me, would go, too. Then I would take my pillow and lie like a little dog at the top of the stairs waiting for someone to come to me.

After this, for me, rather soporific interlude in Newport (I had become accustomed to more exotic things) we were ordered to Peking. Granny cried and said that it was a terrible thing, but Grandfather was all for it. We stayed with them in Washington before leaving and Grandfather bought a small Chinese gong and some Chinese flags and lanterns and adopted a Spartan attitude toward our separation. Mother seemed bewildered but Father, being an old China hand (though never before in Peking), reassured us that our life would be delightful. He sang a song:

> If the day it had been finer,
> You would have seen the Wall of China,
> If it weren't for the housetops
> In between.

All the way across the continent I strained my eyes trying to look over the housetops we passed to see if I could discover China. But almost the only thing that I saw was the heavy black smoke of the engines, which came through the window screens and settled on everything. We sailed from San Francisco, spent a day in Honolulu, and then went on to Yokohama.

Japan was the first glimpse that Mother and I had of the Orient, and we loved it. I was charmed by the children on stilts, the rickshaws, the gaudy temples, the great Kamakura Buddha, the bamboo forests, and some of Father's old geisha friends in the teahouse. The latter were very pretty and greeted Father with birdlike cries and giggled and pawed Mother. We sat on a mat while they made tea for us, which took so long that I fell asleep. It was very impolite but the sightseeing had exhausted me. It was chrysanthemum time and we saw scenes from Japanese history, looking like beautiful tapestries but all made of different-colored chrysanthemums. The scent was delicious, so clean and pungent. It was the thing I liked best about Japan.

It was in Yokohama that Father said he needed some money and must go to the bank. I asked if I could go with him because I had never seen a bank and did not know what it was. It looked a rather dull place when we got there. Father took out a piece of paper called a letter of credit and gave it to a man who took it away. "What is he going to do?" I asked. "Where has he gone to?" "He is going to pick some money off the money tree," said

Father. "The money tree?" I repeated wonderingly. "Yes," said Father, "every bank has a money tree and we have to come here to get it."

I looked around. The bank did not seem a dull place anymore. It seemed mysterious, like one of the Japanese temples. And these men hurrying to and fro seemed like priests. I held on to Father's hand. Where was this tree? What magic came from it? "Does it just grow?" I whispered.

The man came back at that moment and Father did not answer, as he was busy putting the money in his wallet. When he had finished, he gave my hand a big tug and pulled me along. "But Father," I said, "can't I see the money tree?" "No," answered Father firmly. "The only people who can see it are the men who belong to the bank." I fell silent, as I knew from his tone that there was nothing more to be got out of him. Grown-ups had such strange ideas. They liked to talk about dull things such as "Are your hands clean?" and "Did you meet any little friends on your walk?" But give them an exciting topic like a money tree and they had nothing to say.

After that, I went with Father to the bank whenever I could, hoping to see a door open or in some way catch a glimpse of this magic, mysterious thing. But the bank men were fast on their feet and quick as lightning, so I was never able to catch one off guard.

In Shanghai we went directly to the Astor House. "The finest service in the world," Father had told us. "There is a boy at every door." When we went up to our rooms I saw a long, long hall with a man dressed in a white skirt and blue jacket beside every second door. "Who are all these men?" I asked Father. "They are the 'boys,'" he answered. "And when you want your breakfast or your tea, just open the door and tell them."

Father and Mother had so many friends in Shanghai and went out so much that they engaged a Chinese amah to stay with me. I liked her the moment I saw her. She had a heart-shaped face and small, bright eyes and smooth black hair which

WISHING

—poem from my early diary

Oh but that I had wings and
*   could*
* soar like a bird so high*
Out from this sordid earth
*   into*
* the wondrous sky.*

Could see the moon by night,
*   and see the sun by day*
And watch the clouds as they
*   float*
about the great north wind
*   at play*

IN JAPAN SO FAR AWAY

*—written in my Peking
diary at about age seven*

*In a lovely meadow nearby
Where the grass was green,
        and tender
Underneath the sapphire sky,
Dwelt Amaguchi flower-
        vendor
In Japan so far away*

*One day there came to
        Willow-pool
Amaguchi, flowers, and stool.
He did sit beside the water
And talk to Nakaroomi's
        daughter
In Japan so far away.*

*They to a neighboring priest
        did go
And they were united so,
Amaguchi, flower-vendor,
Hana San, so sweet, and
        tender.
In Japan so far away.*

*Of this heard the raging
        parent
So, like a Fire-God he came
Asked her if she would repent
Of her deep and direful
        shame
In Japan so far away.*

she wore in a knot at the back and with a black band of silk in front. We took long walks along the Bubbling Well Road, which led to the racecourse and which was always crowded with carriages and rickshaws. The walk I liked best, though, was to go down to the Bund, or waterfront, and over to the river, because there one saw the sampans all tied together—tiny, fragile-looking little boats, each one with a family aboard, and so crowded that one wondered why they did not sink. Amah explained that these were the only houses the people had because they were very, very poor. They certainly looked it and I was both fascinated and upset.

"Why is that little girl so thin?" I asked Amah. "No have money buy food," she answered. "These coolie all time hungly. No can catchee good bowl rice." "Can't her father go to the money tree?" I demanded. Amah did not understand, so I had to explain to her. Amah laughed. "No let poor coolie in bank," she said, "only foreigners."

This seemed a terrible thing to me and I bombarded my parents with questions that night. Father was tying his evening tie and Mother was powdering her shoulders, and they only laughed and said, "Wait until you are Grown-up and you will understand it."

After a week in Shanghai we boarded a boat which was to take us up the Yangtze River to Tientsin. Amah, much to my joy, had agreed to come with us to Peking. The trip took us several days, as we had to stop and unload cargo, and the villages we passed were fascinating. Everyone came down to watch the ship dock. I grew to know the types: the coolies stripped to the waist, their blue trousers tightly bound around their ankles; the water coolies balancing their buckets across their shoulders on long bamboo poles; the families in their high-wheeled covered carts rattling uncomfortably over the terrible roads; the upper classes, in those days still in sedan chairs.

At one village a play was in progress. A stage had been built in an open spot of the village and the actors performed without scenery or props. All the actors were men and wore masks. One actor, dressed as a woman, wore such a frightful mask with great red horns sticking from it that I shrieked when I saw him. "Amah," I cried, "who is that terrible devil?" "No devil," answered Amah, laughing, "honorable mother-in-law."

It was on the ship that I did a frightful thing. There was a great Manchu prince on board, Prince W., a man of ten thousand characters (the greatest scholar) and of enormous political influence in Peking. He had an entourage of six and they spent most of their time walking round and round the deck conversing in low tones. I watched them, fascinated. They wore long silk robes with short padded-silk jackets and small caps with large jewel-buttons on the top. But what interested me most were their pigtails. They were fat and glossy and long, reaching well below their knees, with beautifully colored tassels on the end. The prince's was the finest. Just above the tassel a jewel gleamed and shimmered as he walked. Then, too, his walk was a little different. His pigtail moved slowly, like a pendulum, with each step. I often followed them from a respectful distance, gazing my fill and utterly absorbed in the rhythm, color, and texture of these extraordinary braids. Gradually I became the prey of an unholy desire. And one day my desire subdued my reason. I darted out from behind a door to give a hearty tug to the prince's pigtail as he rounded the corner. The party stopped and the prince's companions turned on me, furious.

I did not wait for discussion but ran to the family's cabin, where I burst into tears and told my parents all. They were furious, too, and I was about to be locked in my cabin for the rest of the day when a boy came with a message that the prince would like to see Father.

"Well," said Mother, "we have made an enemy before we have even reached Peking. Such an important man, too. Whatever got into you, Brooke!" I howled anew, terribly ashamed and sorry I had done something that was bad for my family. I sat silent on Father's bunk while Mother filed her nails, saying over

Foaming over with his wrath
He chose for her a direful
path
For with his own lips her
heart he stung
Saying, "he would have
Amaguchi hung"
In Japan so far away.

When the moon rose pale
and from high
In the dark and mournful
sky
In the deep and sullen water
Plunged Nakaroomi's lovely
daughter
In Japan so far away!

Next morning all was dark,
and gray
While rain fell from the sky
Amaguchi he did pray
While Nakaroomi she did
die
In Japan so far away.

and over again, "I really can't understand why you should be so terribly naughty."

Father returned wreathed in smiles and kissed Mother, then sat down and let me sit on his lap. "Prince W. was extraordinarily nice," he said. "It is my first experience with the Chinese sense of humor and I would like to go on record by saying that I think it is magnificent. The prince thought the whole thing very funny and that Brooke is a child with a great deal of initiative. He wants to meet her at teatime and has sent her this." And Father gave me a little brocade purse with the prince's crest on it. It was the beginning of a beautiful friendship. We saw a lot of the prince in Peking and, needless to say, I doted on him.

Finally we reached Tientsin and took the train to Peking. When we arrived in Peking we looked out the train window and there on the platform we saw a great crowd. Drawn up and facing us were officers of all the legations' guards dressed in full uniform. In those days, officers' uniforms were really gay and smart and the flash of brass and silver was almost blinding. "I wonder what important person they are meeting?" said Father. We soon found out. As Father in his civilian clothes stepped onto the platform, the ranking American officer came forward to salute him, saying, "Welcome to Peking." Then, while the Marine band struck up, Father was introduced to all the other commandants. It was a wonderful start to our tour of duty in China.

After greetings and handshakes and smiles, we were put into rickshaws and off we sped. In Shanghai I had only been in a double rickshaw with either Mother or Amah. But this time I was alone. My coolie was the fastest and we soon outstripped the others. I was very frightened as we dashed through the crowds. They were different-looking people, much taller and wilder than the people in Shanghai. The streets were much narrower than any I had ever seen and were overshadowed by the huge wall. It seemed such a long way from the station that I was beginning to wonder if my coolie was running away with me. Then we turned into a paved street and, there in front of us, I

. . . the villages. . . were fascinating. Everyone came down to watch the ship dock. I grew to know the types: the coolies stripped to the waist, their blue trousers tightly bound around their ankles; the water coolies balancing their buckets across their shoulders on long bamboo poles; the families in their high-wheeled covered carts rattling uncomfortably over the terrible roads; the upper classes, in those days still in sedan chairs.

saw my own dear flag and the Marines at a large gate. We went in and stopped before a big gray stone house. This was to be our home for the next three and a half years.

Father arrived almost immediately after me, and the first thing he said was, "Brooke, you cannot have anything unless you ask for it in Chinese. If you learn to speak Chinese, you can have everything you want." With this incentive, it did not take me long. In three months I could jabber away in coolie and hold interminable conversations with anyone who would talk to me.

Chapter 5

Peking Pageantry

When we came into our house that first day, a seemingly vast number of Chinese were lined up to greet us. They were dressed in long blue robes with white jackets and they all bowed low when we entered. A tall man at the head of the line came forward and said, "Welcome, Master," to Father. Father gave him a smile and turned to the officer who was accompanying us. "Who are all these people?" he asked. "They are your house servants," said the captain. "I thought you would want to keep on the same staff that Major T. had." Mother looked aghast. "Heavens," she cried, "we are not used to living like this." And Father said, "Great scott, T. must be a millionaire!"

The captain laughed. "With the exchange," he said, "they won't cost more than two people at home. This is Li Wong, your Number One Boy, who will run the house for you."

The No. 1, who had greeted Father, now turned and bowed to Mother. "Welcome, Missy," he said, and to me, "Welcome, Little Girl." He then proceeded to introduce No. 2 Boy, No. 3 Boy, Cook, No. 2 Cook, two make-learn cooks, a rice cook, and several small boys. There were also two Chinese maids and three laundry boys. (We, of course, already had Amah, who had come from Shanghai with us to be a personal maid.)

Father and Mother were overwhelmed by such a retinue, but within a short time after our arrival a resident tailor was added to the household, and a small boy who did nothing but walk my dogs when I was busy with my lessons. On the outside there were six rickshaw coolies (two for each rickshaw) and then, as the family realized how far their money would go, there was a horse for each of us with three grooms to look after them. Father even took to polo and had four polo ponies.

It was certainly not the way in which we had lived at home—this was the life of very rich people—but we soon grew accustomed to it and, when I learned to speak Chinese, I took great delight in the complicated strata of the household staff. I used to love to go into the kitchens and laundries, which were always teeming with life. The servants' kitchen and laundry were sep-

(previous page)
The American legation under the Tienanmen entrance to the Great Wall of Peking. Tienanmen Square is just beyond the gate.

arate from ours, and the rice cook and laundry boy, surrounded by relatives, held forth supreme in these domains. No. 1 Boy was really a steward, as he had the right to hire and fire and all the responsibilities of the household were on his shoulders. He kept the accounts, allocated the work, and superintended Cook's menus. He also was entitled to "squeeze," which was a commission on everything bought for the house. Mother led a life entirely free of any care and was as happy as a lark. Father even had a song to express our delight: "I'm livin' easy on po'k chops greasy. I'm livin' easy, I'm livin' high."

It took us a little while to settle in because soon after we arrived Mother and I became very sick. A doctor who had vaccinated us against smallpox in Shanghai had infected us and we ran a high fever with delirium. There were no antibiotics in those days and only wonderful nursing care and fine constitutions pulled us through. When we finally felt well enough to totter out, we set forth in rickshaws, guided by Father, to view the city.

Peking at that time was still the Imperial City, the home of what was to be the last of the Manchus. The empress dowager (*not* the great empress dowager but the mother of Pu-yi, now Mr. Henry Pu-yi* and a creature of the Communists) was on the throne and all the ceremony and tradition of the imperial past held Peking in thrall. As Dr. Lin Yutang, the Chinese philosopher and writer, said to me, "You were living in Peking in a fascinating period because Peking at that time was twenty-five years behind the rest of China, and China was twenty-five years behind the West."

As we went out that first day it was like stepping back into another age. We went down Legation Street first, the long street that ran under the Tatar Wall from the Tienanmen Gate to the Hata Mên Gate, on either side of which were the high gray walls of the legations. Each legation gate had a guardhouse and a sen-

... when I learned to speak Chinese, I took great delight in the complicated strata of the household staff. I used to love to go into the kitchens and laundries, which were always teeming with life.

*Henry Pu-yi was the last emperor of China. His reign marked the end of the two-thousand-year-old imperial system.

The legation guard parading for the British officers around the central courtyard of the legation.

try pacing back and forth in front of the entrance while above the gate waved the flag of that nation. There were not many Chinese on the streets, as those who came into the Legation Quarter were mostly people on business or those attached in some way to the various legations. Passing through the gate that ended the Legation Quarter, we were out on the Hata Mên, one of Peking's great thoroughfares. What a wonderland was before our eyes! The buildings themselves were of gray stone, as was all of Peking, but it was the shops that were gay beyond belief—lacquer red and celestial blue and bright green, trimmed with gilded fretwork. The shop signs were like banners with red and gold characters painted on colored backgrounds. The shops themselves were marvelous: cabinetmakers and jewelers, shops with antiques and silks, and here and there a teashop and restaurant. We bowled down the middle of the thoroughfare in our rubber-tired rickshaws, gaping at the teeming life around us. The shops were set quite far back from the street proper, and between us and them was what might have been called a sidewalk (all packed dirt, of course) on which itinerant vendors had set up their stalls. There were barbers and letter writers and vendors selling toys and cheap cottons and hundreds of household items. But most fascinating to us were the food vendors. The foods were appetizing and pretty: roasted chestnuts and candied apples threaded on long bamboo poles, little oatmeal cakes being fried in syrup over red-hot braziers, soups with hard-boiled eggs floating on top, stews and fried noodles and small, smooth honey cakes. The smell of cooking was delicious and I immediately begged to be allowed to have a candied apple. Father, whose rickshaw was next to mine, said no, and I did not mind too much when I saw the vendor blow his nose in his fingers and then pick one of the apples from the pole.

The traffic down the middle of the road was terrific. There were high-tilted Peking carts, sedan chairs, rickshaws, and small closed carriages. People did not like to give way to each other because, if they did, it would involve "loss of face," so carts and rickshaws and chairs were constantly being turned over as their wheels grazed each other. Terrible arguments and rows ensued. As Father quipped, "If your face is cracked, it might as well be broken.' "

The only people who really forced their way through the throng were the mandarins. There were at that time nine ranks of mandarins, each man's rank being denoted by the color of the jewel on his cap. They rode in the closed carriages and were entitled, according to rank, to a number of outriders dressed in liveries to match the jewel in the cap of their master. These outriders, who could number up to twelve, rode on their shaggy little Mongolian horses in front of and alongside the carriages. They had long whips with which they lashed out à la cowboy in order to clear the way, and they shouted in strident tones, "Make way, make way for a Highborn Man."

That day on the Hata Mên our coolies shouted back (as we learned later), "We have a Highborn Family here," and refused to budge. When a whip almost grazed Father's cheek, he became furious and yelled to his coolie, who understood English, "Move over, you darned fool!" The coolie gave an order and we moved the tiniest bit so that the mandarin could dash by, his carriage swaying wildly and the servants hanging precariously to a step in the rear while grinning at us triumphantly.

After Father and I learned to speak Chinese, this never happened again. We did not wish to lose face, but when we saw or heard a carriage coming, we automatically said to the coolie, "Move over," thereby averting a contest of rank.

That first day we returned to the legation by way of the Chinese City and the Chien Mên Gate. The narrow hutungs (lanes)

When we finally felt well enough to totter out, we set forth in rickshaws, guided by Father, to view the city.... We bowled down the middle of the thoroughfare in our rubber-tired rickshaws, gaping at the teeming life around us.

were barely wide enough for two rickshaws and were literally teeming with people. There were men going through the streets at a dogtrot, balancing bamboo poles on their shoulders on either end of which was everything from water jars and cement and milk and tiles to crates of geese and chickens and little stunted fir trees. There were men with covered birdcages, and teapots, and huge bundles of blue cloth containing furs or silks or rugs. And there were women (Chinese and Manchu) and children and donkeys and soldiers and, everywhere, beggars—beggars with great red gaping holes instead of eyes and beggars with skin diseases and beggars with legs or arms off and beggars just lying in the gutters too weary to move. The contrast between rich and poor was obvious even to a child. It was a very cold day (it was November) and we were warmly tucked under fur lap robes with fur caps on our heads. The mandarins and the people in the Peking carts and sedan chairs also were warmly wrapped, but many of the people in the street were in rags and shaking visibly from the cold. Though it upset me to see so many poor people, it was all so novel and exciting that my curiosity outweighed my compassion. A brocaded sedan chair, a gaily painted Peking cart, a Manchu lady with her huge headdress and painted face were enough to thrill me.

On this same ride I saw a beggar lying very, very still in the gutter and then, right in front of us, a rickshaw coolie dropped gasping between the shafts. Our coolie skirted the fallen man expertly, but when I glanced back I saw that he looked very strange. "What is the matter with that man?" I asked Father. "He is sick," Father answered. "Will the doctor come?" I said. Father nodded. "Of course." I felt, though, that this was no ordinary illness.

During the years of our life in Peking I grew accustomed to this sight, particularly during the Great Famine and the bubonic plague. I learned it was death, but it did not frighten me again. In this great teeming multitude, death was like a pebble thrown into a pond—the crowd closed around and it was as though it had never been.

As I grew accustomed to death, so I grew accustomed to many exotic sights that were part of the life of the city: a caravan of camels in the compound, Russian Cossacks tearing across their parade ground hanging by one foot from the saddle to pick up a sword with their teeth, Mongolians from the North racing through the streets yelling savagely. These things all became quite ordinary, part of the décor, and did not distract my attention long from my dolls and dogs.

There was one event, though, that stands apart in my memory and that I shall never forget. That was the funeral of the empress, which occurred about six months after our arrival in Peking. Accustomed as I was by then to the pageantry and color of Chinese life, this was something so spectacular that it transcended all other images and scenes.

The empress had died a year before, but the arrangements for the funeral were complicated and had only now been completed. I felt, in a way, that I knew the empress, vicariously, through Mother. A week or two before the empress's death, Mother had been taken by Mrs. Calhoun (the wife of the American minister to China) to be presented at an informal audience. The empress received them in one of the smaller halls. Seated on a golden chair on a slightly raised platform, she wore the high T-shaped headdress of the Manchus, which was festooned with pearls and white jade. She held a handkerchief in her fantastically long-nailed hands, which were ornamented with black and white pearl rings. Beside her on a table lay an enormous scepter of jade—a symbol of her power. As she sat there, acknowledging introductions with a nod of her head, the sun came through the screen behind her and lit up the beautiful translucent green of the scepter. Its reflection turned the empress's haggard face a strange, unearthly green. Mother said it sent a shiver down her spine to look at her. It was "like someone returning from the dead." Later, at the time of the empress's death, when we heard the rumor that she had been poisoned by having crushed diamonds put into her food, Mother was con-

There were men with covered birdcages, and teapots, and huge bundles of blue cloth containing furs or silks or rugs. And there were women (Chinese and Manchu) and children and donkeys and soldiers and, everywhere, beggars...

*My father showing a British officer around
the interior of Tienanmen Gate*

*Mother, her friend Mrs. de Menacol, and my
friend Anna. I'm hiding behind my mother
because my dress had a spot on it,
and I didn't want to be photographed.*

vinced that it was so. Of course I thought so too. I wrote in my diary: "Some say the Empress died a natural death but *I* think she was poisoned."

All this gave me a personal interest in viewing her funeral. Who knew if she might not suddenly rise up out of her coffin and denounce her murderers!

It was to be an all-day affair and, luckily for us, on its route from the Imperial City to the railway station (the empress was to be buried in the North with her ancestors), the procession would pass through the Chien Mên Gate, which was the gate in the wall directly behind our legation. We therefore sallied forth early, armed with sandwiches and soup, for the front-row seats reserved for us on the wall. The wall was fifty feet high, so we got a magnificent view not only of the procession but of the immense crowd that lined the street. The Chien Mên Gate faced directly across to the huge gate in the pink wall of the Forbidden City, and we therefore saw the procession as it emerged from the gate and started toward us. The noise of the procession itself was almost earsplitting; the shouts of the mourners and the clanging of cymbals, and the accompanying murmurs of the crowd were like waves beating against a shore.

Slowly and majestically, to this strange mixture of sounds, the procession advanced, and all day it passed beneath us through the gate. There were Buddhist and Taoist priests in white robes and Buddhist lamas in yellow with red sashes. There were endless bands of eunuchs dressed in white, who tossed paper money in the air (for the empress's use on her way to heaven), and there were court attendants with long yellow feathers in their hats guarding the palanquins that housed the seals and symbols of the power of the empress. There were twenty-four white camels, with yellow brocade tents on their backs (also for her journey), and a whole company of white ponies led by their mafoos, and companies of cavalry and infantry incongruously carrying the flag of the New Republic. There were enormous papier-mâché replicas of all the empress's palaces, and huge trays of fruit and cakes, and sedan chairs of imperial yellow brocade filled with flowers. There were Peking carts in the imperial colors, too, and there were attendants carrying fans and lanterns and copies of great jewels. All this passed accompanied by the cries of the mourners, who tore their hair and beat their breasts to the clashing of cymbals.

The wall of the legation. From the wall we watched the empress dowager's funeral. The funeral was held one year after her death.

We had been hearing a sound like that of a wounded dinosaur. As it eventually drew near, we saw that it emanated from a huge horn borne on the shoulders of twelve men in white with yellow sashes. At certain intervals, a musician blew a long ceremonial wail, which was most eerie. I hung on to Father's arm when I heard it. "It is to drive devils away," explained one of the language officers. As the horn passed under the gate, the wail echoed and reechoed against the walls, and seemed to run right up my legs and into my heart. I hid my face in Father's coat sleeve and Father shook me gently. "Look, Little Woman," he said, "here comes the empress."

I looked down on the huge bier, a mountain of yellow brocade embroidered with red phoenixes (dragons were for an emperor, said the language officer, phoenixes for an empress). It must have been terrifically heavy, as the eighty men who carried it on long poles laid across their shoulders staggered as they walked. All around the bier itself walked hundreds of eunuchs, who were protecting the empress's privacy in death as they had in life.

"Was she very fat?" I asked the language officer. "No," he laughed, "but the box she is in is heavy because it is filled with things she will need on her journey to heaven—food, pillows, cooking utensils, and so forth." That a dead person had to have all these possessions made sense to me. How could any woman travel without the things she knew and prized?

"Do all those paper palaces we saw go in the grave?" I asked. "No, they are burned," he answered, "and the smoke goes up to heaven and makes itself into the houses again."

I looked at the bier passing just beneath us. What fun the empress was going to have! But then I thought about her being poisoned. "Who did it?" I asked. "Who gave her the chopped-up diamonds?" The language officer shrugged. "We don't even know if it's true," he said. "She may have had appendicitis." I discarded that idea at once. There was a mystery about poisoning; it sounded like a fairy story. An ordinary death seemed pretty dull.

At the age of eight I knew that everyone who died went directly to heaven, where God (the American Buddha, as I told Amah) was waiting for him. In heaven everyone was happy and good and did as he pleased, so it was lovely to be there, but the way of getting there was less clear. The Chinese made much of it and seemed to think it was a Good Thing. But Grown-ups spoke of it as something terrible and looked very sad if one of them was taken. All of this was very confusing, particularly as few people in *my* Grown-up world died but it was always happening to the Chinese.

Chapter 6

A Worm's-Eye
View of Life

There is something romantic about living in a walled city. Peking was composed of three walled cities—the Chinese City, the Forbidden City, and the Imperial City. The Legation Quarter hugged the Tatar Wall, which enclosed the Chinese City, and the first thing we saw on awakening in the morning was the huge wall looming above the walls of the compound. I understand that the Communist government has torn down the Peking walls and, much as I dislike the thought of these beautiful and historic monuments being lost to future generations, still I can understand the psychology—walls keep things in. They also keep things out.

The foreigners in Peking were as much influenced by the walls as were the Chinese. The walls of Peking shut out the world that they knew and so they created a never-never land of their own, which was quite dissociated from real life. Herded as they were together in the rather cramped Legation Quarter, seeing one another continually, they set out to fight ennui with the intensity of a Walter Reed tracking down a mosquito. (It must be remembered that during that time a revolution was going on in China and a European war was hanging over our heads.) From the morning, when they started off on rides or picnics, to the evening, when the lanterns, with the host's name in great red characters to guide the rickshaw coolies, were put outside the houses, there was constant activity. Expeditions, bridge parties, receptions, thés dansants, dinners, cotillions, and private theatricals—all kept the Legation Quarter humming. Paris and London were far away, but by every post came reminders of them. Packages poured in—everything from the latest books and periodicals to Paris dresses and hats and canaries from the Harz Mountains to be given as cotillion favors. It was a glorious life and Mother entered into it with all her zest and joie de vivre.

She soon became the belle of Peking and no party was complete without "the Russells." It was quite a compliment because the "inner circle" of Peking European society was a highly civilized, highly intelligent group. These people amused themselves inordinately but they refused to tolerate stupidity or dullness of wit. One had to be on one's toes intellectually and, of course, completely bilingual, as French and English were used interchangeably. Thanks to Henry May's wide range of knowledge and exquisite taste, Mother had kept up with the latest French and English writers and some of the more esoteric writers of the past, and so was quite prepared to enter into the Peking life of the mind. Father did not have the same intellectual interests as Mother (no dissecting of *Une Femme de Trent Ans* for *him*), but he was an excellent bridge player, a good horseman, and superb at tennis. He refused to act, and dances bored him. But he had a shrewd, dry sense of humor and was endowed with the wonderful quality of being a good listener. He was also a top man in his profession and, as there were many officers in Peking, he had hosts of friends with interests similar to his. Together Mother and Father were a most attractive and acceptable couple.

One of their activities that interested me enormously was a group called "The Purple Cows." It was supposed to be a literary society and was composed of the French minister and Madame de Margery (she was the sister of Edmond Rostand, the author of *Chantecler*, etc.), the Americans Mr. and Mrs. Daniel de Menocal, Mr. and Mrs. Willard Straight (she was Dorothy Whitney of New York), the French banker Casenave, and a couple of others whom I did not know so well. The idea of calling the society the Purple Cows emanated from Mr. Straight. Monsieur Casenave sent to Paris for purple Charvet dressing gowns with orange collars and cuffs that the male members wore over their suits at meetings, with impressive effect. When the meeting was held at our house, I used to peek in to watch as they sat around in a circle reading aloud.

Every member was expected to compose a paper to be read at the meetings. They could write on any subject they chose. I knew that Mr. Straight could both write and illustrate and that the de Margerys and Casenave were gifted writers. Mother could always dash off something and, when she read it herself,

Picnicking in the Western Hills with Mother, my amah, and an orderly

make it sound particularly attractive. But I was dubious about Father's ability! Finally, I got up the courage to ask him, "What do you write about for the Purple Cows, Father?" I was sitting on the floor watching him buckle on his sword for a parade when I put the question to him.

"Damn," said Father as the sword banged against his leg. Then, looking me straight in the face, "War," he said sternly.

"War!" I exclaimed. "Do you write about war every single time?"

"Yes," replied Father, "every single time. How to make war and how to avoid it." My head reeled. This was Father in a new light, half Saint George, half dragon, breathing fire intermittently! It thrilled me.

Even though writing of war, Father was not always thinking of it. He took a Chinese lesson every day and when we left Peking could not only speak fairly good Mandarin but could also write it. He knew many Chinese people and was tremendously interested in learning all he could of their psychology and customs. Father also spoke adequate Japanese and went often to stag dinners at the Japanese legation.

It was at one of these dinners in 1913, during a lull in the conversation, that Father looked down at the Japanese imperial crest on his dinner plate—a beautiful chrysanthemum. It was in orange and gold and should have had twelve petals for the twelve provinces. In idly counting the petals, however, Father found thirteen. He thought it must be a mistake, and out of curiosity counted the petals on the dinner plates on either side of him. Those chrysanthemums, too, had thirteen petals. He looked up at that moment and caught his host's eye.

"A penny for your thoughts, Major," laughed the Japanese commandant.

"I notice," replied Father, "that these chrysanthemums have thirteen petals. It is *most* interesting." The commandant looked furious and for a moment there was a silence. Then the Japanese started to make raucous conversation all at once. When the next

Naturally, for me the best fun in Peking was the worm's-eye view I had of the Grown-ups' life. As I was around so much I had a good chance to observe them. I found them utterly fascinating and they were a constant inspiration to me for the copybooks that I was filling with stories, plays, and poems.

course was served, the plates had twelve-petal chrysanthemums.

Father told Mother about it the next afternoon at teatime. "The victory plates were brought out by mistake," he said. "I am sure that there will be the devil to pay with their Number One Boy." "What do you mean by 'victory plates'?" asked Mother. "They obviously intend to annex Manchuria," said Father. "I have been wondering just when they were going to do it."

The Japanese *did* annex Manchuria, as we all know, and little Pu-yi became the puppet emperor of Manchukuo.

Father, in other words, kept his eyes open while he mingled with the Chinese, foreign diplomats, and fellow officers. He was far from headquarters and had to make many decisions on his own. His initiative may, in fact, be one of the reasons he was chosen to be high commissioner to Haiti and major general commandant of the Marine Corps. The Peking life, as you can see, offered a great deal to my family, and both Mother and Father got out of it just what was needed to enlarge their horizons and add luster to their personalities. It was an Edwardian life in an eighteenth-century atmosphere. For me it was the normal Grown-up world. I sensed intrigue around me but it was masked in discretion. I heard talk that I did not understand and I saw things that made no sense. The climate of the society was effete but distinguished. As a result, I became quite sophisticated but absurdly innocent—a rather ridiculous combination.

Naturally, for me the best fun in Peking was the worm's-eye view I had of the Grown-ups' life. As I was around so much I had a good chance to observe them. I found them utterly fascinating, and they were a constant inspiration to me for the copybooks that I was filling with stories, plays, and poems. I used to hide these literary efforts under the sofa or behind my fur-lined boots in the closet because Mother was very interested in reading them.

When I was five or six and wrote baby poems like

I had a little cat and it slept upon a mat
All day long and purred its song,

The cover of my diary from 1911. It is titled "Philosophies of a Child or The Study of Human Nature in General 1911" and it is dedicated to "Imagination." Note the admonishment: "Gentle reader, be not too severe!"

then I had wanted to show them to Mother, but as my efforts became more ambitious I became more sensitive to criticism. Mother was highly critical. When in a poetic drama I wrote "the Duke called to his musicians and said, 'What ho, my Booms and Bastrums there, Strike up a lively, tuneful air,' " it cut Mother to the quick. "If you intend to write," she said, "you must at least learn the English language. Study your Thesaurus. This sounds disgusting," and, taking a pencil, she struck out those resonant words "Booms and Bastrums" and wrote in "Viols and Bassoons." I had dedicated the play "To Imagination" and felt that, even though I was only nine, I was entitled to a little poetic license. Anyway, to me my *own* words sounded better and I was certain that Booms and Bastrums existed as musical instruments.

King Arthur and the Knights of the Round Table and *Froissart's Chronicles* inspired many of my stories. My hero was apt to be on a "coal-black charger with trappings of purest gold." He was usually out searching for dragons and wicked people, but in his moments of dalliance he said things very reminiscent of the American Bachelors' Kocktail Club, or of Mother's friends Messieurs di Lucca, Casenave, Pelakin, and Luxburg. He was truly a work of art—part Marine, part accomplished ladies' man. The heroine, who was always incredibly beautiful, simply smiled or wept, depending upon the situation. When eventually I got tired of those characters I branched out into a "modern novel." It was the story of a charming young girl (very, very poor) and also rather old (almost nineteen) and a duke. In it there was an episode where the duke came to call on the girl. His manners do not seem to have been of the best, or perhaps he felt that his position in life entitled him to speak as he pleased, because when he entered the drawing room where the girl was sitting on the sofa he said, "Who was that hideous old hag who opened the door for me?" The girl, without a moment's hesitation, said, "Oh, that old crone. She is the cook."

Actually the crone was the girl's mother.

This was a story I usually kept hidden from Mother's eyes, but one day I left it carelessly on top of my desk. When I returned from school, there she was, in the chair by the stove, reading it. She rose to her feet when she saw me and dramatically waved the copybook in my face. "You ungrateful child!" she cried. "What is going on in your mind? It breaks my heart that you should even imagine that a girl would deny her mother. Besides, you are a horrid little snob," and, opening the stove door, she flung the copybook into the fire and strode out of the room.

Stoically I watched it burn. It was not one of my best efforts. I knew in my heart that the duke and the girl were far from being nice characters and I had not been sure what I was going to do about them. Now it was settled. What I found inconsistent, though, was that Mother thought me a snob. I was making the characters in the story snobs because they were *not* nice people. Mother was constantly saying that I liked only dreary, inferior children and I never bothered with the really chic ones. How, then, could she think me a snob? Just because the girl and the duke were snobs did not mean that I was one. *I* was a writer.

Although trained to do what I was told and perfectly willing to follow the pattern, still I became more and more conscious that Grown-ups were not infallible. It was a disturbing thought. I did not like it. I did not want to sail the uncharted seas alone. I wanted a wise and sympathetic pilot, as without one I knew that I would founder.

Most of my knowledge of Grown-ups was gained from lingering in the drawing-room doorway when I was summoned down to make my round of curtsies at teatime. But occasionally I participated actively in their life, though I could only join them in the daytime activities, as I had to be in bed by eight.

The thing I liked best of all were the picnics, and the best picnics were the winter ones, which were really delicious. My favorite place was the Princess Tombs. We used to skate out on the frozen canals, arriving at the tombs in time for lunch. These tombs, like all important Chinese tombs, were rows of enor-

The Temple of Heaven. This is the spot from which the emperor viewed the world.

mous stone statues lining a broad road to a temple. The statues represented huge beasts standing guard, looking ferocious and wise. I adored them and felt sure that they danced and played at night when no one was looking. We took off our skates at the landing and walked down to where the table was set in some sheltered place. The boys had come out early in the morning, long before we were up, and brought with them a trestle table, benches, linen, silver, food, and wine. The table was set just as prettily as at home and the food was all piping hot. To keep us warm we had fur rugs over our legs and charcoal braziers between every two people. After the long skate out, in that wonderful clear, cold air, everyone felt marvelously well and in a good humor. There was much jollity and Mother, in particular, seemed to have many witty things to say. I laughed heartily along with Messieurs Casenave, Pelakin, di Lucca, and the others because I did not want to appear "out of it."

When my family gave a picnic I used to exchange glances with No. 1 Boy, knowing how pleased he was to pull off such a fine feast in those circumstances, and I gave him all the encouragement and praise I could in a look. It was a bore when other children were brought along because then I had to talk to them. I much preferred the Grown-ups' talk. The Grown-ups, of course, were very polite and some of them made much of me. One of them even gave me a great red ticket which bore the initials K.T., meaning that I was a member of the American Bachelors' Kocktail Club. I knew it was a joke but I was very pleased and treasured it.

At times the Grown-ups' talk was quite silly, and I knew that if I had said the things they did I would have been told that I was stupid. They acted as though children had no ears and no sense. I made a note in my diary that "Grown-ups like to show off, too." Sometimes Mother wanted me to show off and I tried to play whatever role she assigned me. But there were also times when she definitely did not want to acknowledge my presence, as when she left me to tag along far behind when she went skat-

It was an Edwardian life in an eighteenth-century atmosphere. For me it was the normal Grown-up world. I sensed intrigue around me but it was masked in discretion. I heard talk that I did not understand and I saw things that made no sense.... As a result, I became quite sophisticated but absurdly innocent—a rather ridiculous combination.

ing. I was never quite sure what I was supposed to do.

There were also picnics at the Temple of Heaven and at the racecourse. The picnics at the racecourse were especially exciting, as the races were for gentlemen jockeys and the interest of the onlookers was intense. One gentleman was so gallant that when the husband of the lady he was in love with could not ride, he turned his own horse over to an inferior horseman and rode her horse to win. This caused more excitement than the Revolution and I enjoyed it immensely. It was truly a feat worthy of Sir Lancelot.

There were many trips I did not go on. I never saw the Great Wall of China or the Ming Tombs or the big Lama Temple because they were overnight journeys. I would have been very good, and I wished then, and now more than ever, that I had been allowed to go.

When Amah and I had an afternoon to ourselves we took the dogs walking on the wall, which was a favorite promenade ground for the foreigners. The back gate of our legation was almost parallel to one of the ramps leading to the wall and our Marines guarded the blockhouse over the gate which led to the Chinese City. The wall was about a hundred feet wide and had blockhouses at strategic intervals. The gray blockhouses had red-tile roofs with curving ends and were very pretty.

From the wall, one could see down onto the legations on one side and the Chinese City on the other, then beyond the legations the Chinese City again. Off to the left was the Imperial City with its pink walls surmounted with yellow tiles and, in the middle, the great mass of yellow-tile roofs that was the Winter Palace.

Amah and I liked it particularly at sunset, when the gray stones of the Chinese houses turned to soft mauve pink and the canals beyond the Outer City looked like bits of rosy glass. At

Obviously my grandfather had a very high opinion of me! (Note the British spelling of "Miss.")

A picnic party at the Princess Tombs

*Climbing onto one of the enormous stone horses at the
Princess Tombs with some English friends*

The Purple Cows (so called because the gowns were made, by Charvet, in purple brocade): Mother is in the fur cap at center, Father is to the left of Minister Calhoun (white hair and moustache). Mrs. Calhoun is wearing the white hat at left. Monsieur de Margery (with the dark moustache) was the French minister to Peking—his son later became the French ambassador to the United States. Willard Straight, a banker (upper right), was married to Dorothy Whitney, who is in the dark fur hat behind Monsieur de Margery.

Mr. Somerville, U.S. attaché, with Mother (right) and friend

Mother and Monsieur Casenave (right) along with friends Mr. and Mrs. de Menocal in Peking

Minister Calhoun, Mother (at back), me, and the wife of my doctor

The Great Wall in a photograph taken by my father

this hour the pigeons would fly in formation over our heads. The leader had a wooden whistle tied to his wing which made an eerie sound as he flew. Also at this time the rooks flew in sweeping flocks, cawing vociferously. They always flew in the same direction. "Where are they going?" I asked Amah. "They must hully to get into the Imperial City before the gates close," she answered. "If no can get in, die!" I used to watch them anxiously after that and inwardly urge on the laggards.

The wall was the place where ladies and gentlemen ("Mother's friends") met and walked at odd times of the day. I would report at lunch or tea on whom I had seen. "I saw Monsieur G. and Madame P. walking arm in arm," I said once conversationally. "They were having a lovely time and were looking at each other so much that they never saw me." Father and Mother exchanged a glance and No. 1 Boy moved a step closer. "Don't ever tell whom you see on the wall," said Mother sharply. "Don't tell anyone." "Why not?" I asked, surprised. "Because it's not nice to hear children talking about Grown-ups," replied Mother. This seemed most unfair, that a child could not talk about a Grown-up. Grown-ups had no compunction in talking about children, and right in front of them!

"It is too bad that Brooke has Marion's figure," Mother complained to a friend. (Marion was Father's sister and I knew that Mother thought her a frump.) "Well," the friend answered, "she seems quite bright and I must say you have brought her up beautifully." "Do you think so?" Mother seemed pleased. "Heaven knows I've tried. But she is a moody child and not a bit like the Howards, who are all so gay."

After that remonstrance from Mother I never again mentioned whom I saw on the wall. But I wrote diligently in my diary and I had some fine material handy for causing the breakup of quite a few happy homes, if I had only known it.

It was on the wall that Mother got the compliment which she constantly quoted as being the best she had ever received. She had been very nervous and tired and the doctor ordered her to walk at least five miles a day, rain or shine. She did it for about a week. On one of those days it was raining hard, so she went out in an old high-neck sweater and no hat. She hoped no one else would be out in such weather. But Monsieur N. of the French legation, also under doctor's orders, came face to face with her. He stopped and stared, then bent and kissed her hand. "Madame Russell," he exclaimed ecstatically, "you are so adorably ugly." Father liked neither the kissing of the hand nor the compliment and I wondered what it was all about. It seemed to enchant Mother. "Always remember, Brooke, that a doubtful compliment is the best," said Mother to me. "Just the way a smile is better than a laugh, and a light in the eyes best of all."

It was on the wall that I often ran into Mr. K., the Russian minister, walking with Kitty S., a French girl, about six years older than I. We had met at children's parties and I used to smile and wave at them as we passed. They seemed to be having a good time. And I understood perfectly, as a lot of Father's friends were very nice to me. But I did not understand it when one day at tea Mother said to Father, "It's the most disgusting thing I've ever heard." "He ought to be shot," said Father severely. "I hear she slipped away dressed as a coolie and he took her to Mukden," said Mother, pouring herself another cup. "Scratch a Russian and find a Tatar," said Father. "The Russians aren't really civilized. I never liked old K. I always thought him sly." "But Kitty seemed like such a charming girl," said Mother. "I understand that Mr. S. has gone after them. But once they get into Russia, it will be hopeless."

When I realized whom they were talking about I burst into a hearty laugh. "I'd love to go off with Captain Hopkins dressed as a coolie," I said. (Captain Hopkins was the president of the American Bachelors' Kocktail Club.) Mother glared at me. "Stop showing off," she said. "It's most unattractive. You don't know what you're saying."

And, of course, I really did not.

The house of one of Mother's friends, outside the Legation Quarter, Peking

FIRELIGHT

—written at age nine

How I love thee, firelight,
Glimmering, glittering
*   always bright,*
Never have I failed to see
Pictures, and fancies hidden
*   in thee.*
Many a cold, and dreary day
Have I spent in your welcome
*   ray.*
Oh where do you go oh flames
*   of blue?*
Why, up the chimney, and
*   down the flue.*

A Play by Brooke Russell
Peking, 1911

Dedicated to Imagination

Author's note: This play, written when I was nine years old, was a little offspring of my mother's reading. Mother had been reading me Sir Walter Scott and stories about knights and damsels and dukes and duchesses, and always eager to please her I wrote this play. The childish spelling throughout this play (and in all the following diaries and poems) is my own. To this day I'm a terrible speller. I think because I was taught in Peking to spell the English way (humour and travelling, etc.), I am still mixed up eighty years later!

Scene: Hall or throne room
of the Duke's

Dramatis Persona

Duke Alphonso: duke of Bretagne
Earl of Chester, Hero
Prince Henri Valporiso, villain
courtiers, servants ect.
Duchess of Bretagne
Rosolind: daughter of the duke
Lady Beatrix, Chester's sister
Ladies, maids ect.

Act I

Scene—Duke's Palace
coutiers ect

Duke   "I pray you Lords, and Ladies fair
Where is my daughter where oh where."
I pray you fetch her, Lady Marie
The page, Armondo shall go with thee"

Marie   curtsying
"I go my Lord as you bid me.
And I will find her as you bid me"
(she goes out)

Duke   "What Ho, my boons and bastrums there
Strike up a lively, tuneful air"
(music strikes up)
Enter Marie with Rosolind

Rosolind curtsying
"My Father wishest thou to speak to me
I am here and lo I bow to thee
(bowing)

Duke   "I pray you be seated my daughter dear

And listen to this tale you have to hear
(music stops) Rosolind sits down
      at the Duke's feet

<u>Duke</u>   It is now time my daughter that you'd
look for a ring
"And I have found you a handsome
  prince
Who is the very thing

<u>Rosolind</u>
"I pray you Father what is his name
And is it in the book of fame?

<u>Duke</u>   His name is Henri Vallporiso
And I will you his picture show"
     (draws forth picture)
       smiling
Is he not a comely youth?
He has a manly form in truth"

<u>Rosolind</u> aside
Methinks I've heard that name before
From my beloved Isadore
      aloud
Methinks he has a sinister look
And his nose an uncommon bad hook

<u>Duke</u>   "I trow you look not in scorn
For you will wed the morrow morn"

<u>Roso</u>   aside
"I will not wed tomorrow for
I love my own sweet Isadore
     (faints)

<u>Duke</u>   What Ho she faints my Ladies fair,

Stand back, stand back and give her air
     (Enter duchess)

<u>Duchess</u> Looking around
"Pray what is all this noise about?"
The people yell and the people shout"

<u>Duke</u>   (aside to duchess)
"This is how she acted you know
When I told her about Vallporiso."

<u>Duch.</u> shrieking
"Oh Alphonso, Alphonso
Oh Oh Oh
    (faints) silence on the stage
a litter is brought in Roso. and Duch. are
     carried out

<u>Duke</u>   shaking his head
"It is queer how the Ladies do act nowadays
I really wish that they'd mend these ways
    (He muses)
    (curtain)

Act 2

Scene   Garden, night about 11 o'clock
All is dark, enter Vallporiso cloaked in black

<u>Val</u>   "Rosolind loves me not alack, alack
But I will win her back, yes back.
Away from my old enemy Isadore
And she shall see him never more"

Ha Ha!

Noise at left offstage. Enter Lady Beatrix

Beat.   putting finger to her lips

"Hush, be quiet my darling Love

For Rosolind's room is just above"

she points to light in window of Castle

Beat   "Here is all that we need

To carry out our bloody deed"

She hands him sword and scimiter,

Val   "Come my darling let us hide hear

Why do you tremble? I have no fear"

They hide behind rock

Enter Sir Isadore with guitar

Isadore He looks around

"My lovely Rosolind, she is not here

I will sing, mayhap she will appear"

takes out guitar and starts singing

Song

"Oh Queen of my heart so fair and

bright

The moon shall watch o'er thee by night

The sun shall shine o'er thee by day

And roses sweet shall strew thy way

Oh for a glance of your soft dark orbs

And the whole of my spirit in you

absorbs,

Oh but to touch my lips with thine

Would be far better than any wine.

I wish that now you'd seal my fate

And lead me to Heaven's lofty gate

He stops and looks up at the window.

Rosolind puts her head out and motions him

she's comming out. In a few minutes she

comes out kisses him they look at each-other

and laugh, they sit down on mosy log

Roso   "The days seem long and the nights

seem drear,

When I am not with you my dear,

(She sighs)

Isadore "But my dear one, why should we tarry?

Let us make haste now and marry"

She nods her head they start to go off stage

Val. starts out with knife in hand

Val   mockingly

"Yes, why should you tarry

Why should you not marry?

Isadore turns around draws sword

Roso   "Oh,—oh oh

Vallporiso"

She sobs   only the clinking of the steel is

heard

Roso   "Ah t'is true he has a deadly foe

He gains, ah yes, ah no!"

Isadore runs point of sword through Vallporiso

Roso   "Bravo Bravo my Isadore"

suddenly she sees Beat approaching with knife

from behind

Roso   "Turn, turn Isadore

Turn as I said before

Isadore turns—Beat drops sword

Isa   "Ah all I hear is true
     You would kill me *you!*
       He points finger at her
Beat   "Yes for him, I'd do it and more" she
     points to Val's body
     And *you, you* have killed him Isadore
  She turns away with her head in her arms
     Roso takes Isadore by the arm
Roso "Come we must make haste, make
     haste
     For we must wed and have no time to
     waste
    They go out Isadore looking back
    Beatrix goes other side still crying

        (curtain)

    Scene garden next morning
      Enter Duke with Page

Duke "Vallporiso and my daughter this
     morn shall marry
     T'is getting late why do they tarry"
He starts toward sundial in doing so he stum-
  bles against Val's body He starts back in
     Suprise, Anger and Fear.
Duke "Vallporiso dead—Great Ceasers
     Come forth my stupid fool Eleasers"
He beckons fool. Page is frightened at the sight

starts back but kneels at Dukes feet
Duke "Dost know who did it thou wretched
     fool?
     T'is neatly done for I see no tool"
Jester

     "Nay now Uncle, How should I know
     If it were done by sword, scimiter lance
     or bow"
Duke "Go fetch the court, and my daughter
     also
     Who did this deed, I *must* and will know
      Jester exits making faces
Duke (pacing up and down)
     "What will all his kinsmen say?
     Why, that I killed him the very first day
     Oh that this should fall on me
     What can I do. Oh let me see
       (He stops)
     Ah now I have it the very thing
     He swallowed his own wedding ring
     Ha Ha! isn't that funny
     For I will get all his wedding money
     (Enter court with Lady Roso)
Duke "Come my daughter dost thou know
     About the wretched death of
     Vallporiso?
Roso "Ah yes my Father, I've heard my
     maidens tell,
     That at the present moment He abides
     in Hell

	I know the mur—
Duke	(aghast)
	Daughter, dost thou knowst what thou said
	It shows disrespect to the mourned for dead
Rose	Aye yes I know that and more
	I know the murderer as I said before
Duke	(in suprise)
	You daughter, you know the wretched man
	Who killed this noble prince by his filthy hand
Roso	T'was I who made that proud man stagger
	And I killed him with this bloody dagger
	(draws forth dagger from dress)
Duke	That this should come upon our race
	That *I* should suffer this disgrace
	(He buries his head in his arms)
Isadore	coming out from behind a screen
	"I cannot allow this to go,
	T'was I who killed Valporiso"
	And I did it so I could marry your daughter sweet
	I'm glad to know he has met his defeat
Duke	(looking up)
	Ah! You are the noble youth
	And by my crown I speak the truth
	You are the youth who helped me win

	That wonderful victory of Eckin Glin
	And you shall marry my daughter this very morn
	(turning to Roso)
	Go daughter your wedding gown adorn!"
	(exit Roso)
Duke	All the wedding preparations are made
	And there's only the sermon to be said
	(enter Roso clad in wedding gown)
	(Page brings goblet to duke according to custom)
Duke	"The pope shall pronounce you man and wife
	And here's to a long, and noble life!"
	(He drinks)

Chapter 7

Parties,
Parties,
Parties

While Father and Mother were busy with their life in Peking, they saw to it that I was kept equally busy with mine. To be a child in Peking in 1911–1914 one needed great stamina. I was not terribly strong then and there were moments when I succumbed to a "quinsy" sore throat or a horrid hacking cough brought on by the dust storms. There was not, however, a place in our household for a "lie-a-bed" and, after Mother had read me a chapter from *Les Malheurs de Sophie* or Dora's Dinner Party from *David Copperfield,* I was supposed to be quite cured.

Mother was busy at her desk every morning sending out "chits" for parties at our house or scribbling her answers to invitations in someone else's chit book. Often these chits concerned me, as most of Mother's friends seemed to have children and the desire of the parents of all nationalities was to keep us constantly shuttling back and forth from house to house.

When I returned from school, the plan for the afternoon was given to me. The Japanese legation, the French, the British, the Russian, the Danish, the Austrian, the Hungarian—Amah and I went to them all. I was supposed to be "making friends" and learning how to converse in all the different languages. But what it really boiled down to was something else. With the British children I would burn pictures in wood or hammer brass or do decalcomania, and then we would have cambric tea and bread-and-dripping. With the French I would play "Savez-vous Plantez les Choux" or "Cache, Cache" and drink hot chocolate or white wine and water, and eat tiny éclairs. The Russians had tea and little hot meat pies, the Japanese tea and deliciously sweet waferlike cakes, and so it went. Age seemed to make no difference; one day I was sent to play with a Japanese child of four and the next with a French girl of sixteen, who would not speak to me because she was engrossed in reading a fashion magazine from Paris. I remember this particular girl well because I was sent to her house about three times a winter and always got the same reception. "Soyez gentille," pleaded her governess but Sylvie, shrugging her shoulders, would give me a glance of pity mingled with contempt and would return to her reading. I hated her, as she was not really a Grown-up and so had no right to treat me as though I were nothing.

Our parents had a passion for seeing us in costume, and three or four times a season we appeared at parties dressed according to the theme of the occasion. The British legation was a great center for these parties. I remember one occasion there when all the girls came dressed as flowers and all the boys as insects. Mr. Pat Ramsay, who was a secretary of the legation, was thinly disguised as a gardener and came into the ballroom pushing a wheelbarrow full of presents for us. I was dressed as a rose in a costume made of taffeta petals, shading from pale to dark pink and each petal wired to stand out so that I looked like a round pink ball. On my head was a close-fitting green hat with a long stem sticking from the top of it. Harrison Hatch, age six and three years my junior, was dressed as a ladybug and kept buzzing around me, sticking his tongue out. He was an American boy and did not have the courtly manners of the French or the Russians.

One Christmas a pantomime was put on at the British legation. I took part in it, supposedly as a poor little girl who wandered around in her nightie. (My nightie, made by Tailor for the occasion, was no poor child's nightie but quite spectacular, of the thinnest wool, all smocked and trimmed with real Valenciennes lace.) I was in my nightie because it was Christmas Eve and, alone in my garret, I was wringing my hands and weeping while looking at an empty stocking hung by the mantelpiece. While I wept, my face covered with my hands, a Good Fairy came tripping in, filled the stocking and then, dancing gaily over to me, tapped me with her silver wand. At that moment I was supposed to rise up in a joyous way, undo the buttons of my nightie, and step out of it, revealing myself in a beautiful pale-blue silk dress, complete with pale-blue kid slippers. Anna, a matter-of-fact, down-to-earth girl, the daughter of the doctor attached to the British legation, did her part as the Good Fairy

Our parents had a passion for seeing us in costume, and three or four times a season we appeared at parties dressed according to the theme of the occasion. The British legation was a great center for these parties. I remember one occasion there when all the girls came dressed as flowers and all the boys as insects.

... to celebrate the coronation of George V, a maypole dance was organized on the huge croquet lawn of the British legation.

valiantly. But I, stumbling to my feet with a "joyous smile" fixed on my face, could not undo the buttons. Finally, in desperation I tore them off and, as the nightie dropped to my ankles, my feet became entangled in it and I fell prone in front of Anna. She, with great aplomb, kept on determinedly hitting me with the wand until just as the curtain fell I rose unsteadily to my feet and blew a kiss to the audience instead of making a pirouette in front of Anna, which I was supposed to do.

This episode hurt Mother's pride terribly and she talked for weeks of how incredible it was that a Howard should have no sense of theater or stage presence. "I am afraid that she is all Russell," she said gloomily to her friends. I knew what she meant. The Russells were a good, worthy, substantial lot, ever ready to answer the call of God and Country, but pretty dull at the dinner table.

I was a little more successful when, to celebrate the coronation of George V, a maypole dance was organized on the huge croquet lawn of the British legation. I was one of four older girls to dance, and we rehearsed for weeks. We wore blue pleated dresses and wreaths of forget-me-nots in our hair as, with elephantine grace, we wound the blue ribbons around the pole while the smaller children darted in and out with white ribbons. Given before an audience of parents, governesses, and nannies, this dance was a roaring success and the fact that some ribbons were left flapping was kindly overlooked.

The American legation did not do as much as the British, but I remember one party the Calhouns gave when I went as Priscilla Alden (I had no idea who she was) and was photographed with the ubiquitous Harrison Hatch, who was dressed as Benjamin Franklin at the court of France. It was all very patriotic and must have been amusing to our parents but, as I have said, hard work for the children. Some Chinese children came to the parties, but not many because China was in a state of political unrest and even the officials did not go out much.

Henry Pu-yi was about my age and often sat next to me at parties. He was a nice boy, but shy, and his main interest in life was flying kites, at which he was quite expert. In China flying kites is a great art, attended by many competitions and great rivalry, and I stood a bit in awe of him. I was afraid to fly a kite myself, as they were so enormous and needed great skill to manipulate. I feared that I might be carried right over the walls of Peking. I did, however, learn to race about on stilts. It was great fun to go through the snow on them, and I used to feel like Long John Silver as I raised an angry wooden leg in the air.

In spite of the fact that I was being rushed to visit the children of Mother's friends almost every afternoon and had the chance, as Mother said, to meet so many charming children, I really never cared much for any of them. Everything was so highly organized, under the eyes of governesses and nannies, that there was no chance to find out what the other children were really like. Mother knew I did not enjoy my afternoons. It vexed her and she looked coldly at me one day as I reluctantly set forth to spend the afternoon with two girls, one five years older and the other three years younger than I was.

"Why are you such a stick-in-the-mud?" she exclaimed. "Good heavens, this is a chance of a lifetime for you to mix with these delightful, different nationalities. *I* should think you would appreciate it, instead of looking like a thundercloud. I suppose you would rather have that dreadful alley cat Gwladys here." I turned to go. "I'm late," I muttered. "Brooke," demand-

Henry Pu-yi was about my age and often sat next to me at parties. He was a nice boy, but shy, and his main interest in life was flying kites, at which he was quite expert.

ed Mother sternly, "you are not sulking, are you?" "No, Mother," I answered, my hand on the doorknob. "Well, then," said Mother, turning back to her dressing table, "for heaven's sake be cheerful. Go out and have some fun. If you go out looking sour like that, of course you will have a horrible time."

I waited a moment, dutifully, but she was looking at herself in the mirror, so I fled. Of course Mother was right. I *did* want to be with Gwladys. I knew that my friendship with her annoyed Mother almost beyond endurance and that Father was puzzled by it, but I simply would *not* give Gwladys up. She was my one real friend.

Gwladys was the daughter of an American missionary of Welsh descent. Her parents were not only missionaries (an anathema to my parents) but, worse still, they were "bluestockings" (Mother said a bluestocking was an intelligent bore). They had married late in life and the mother had been a schoolteacher. Even I, doting on Gwladys as I did, could not hold much brief for them. They were a dried-up, dreary, messy-looking couple. Their house was filled with books of all description and Gwladys discussed books and events with her family as though she were a Grown-up and on an equal footing with them. She was nothing much to look at. She had a pasty face, lank black hair, and a rather furtive eye. Nevertheless, the days when I was allowed to ask her over to play were red-letter days for me.

Mother believed that, except in a raging storm, a child should spend at least two hours out of doors during the afternoon. In the circumspect houses I visited, the hours always dragged until teatime came and we could go in. But with Gwladys the time passed on wings. No matter if it was cold enough to have our fur earlaps down or if it was just damp and misty, no matter what, Gwladys could turn it into an enchanted world.

We usually went to a corner of the Guard Compound, where a wall jutted out from the Legation Compound. It was a little bit out of the way and we were not likely to be disturbed. "Now," I would say impatiently when we arrived there, "now, what are we going to play today?" Gwladys would shut her eyes and a look of intense concentration would come over her ratlike face. "Let me see." I would wait for her moment of inspiration and, suddenly, it would come. Gwladys would take a stick and start to draw in the sand. "This is the drawbridge," she would say. "It is gray wood and very old and has teeth of iron that slide down over the gate when it is pulled up. And here is the great hall, and here the tower where the maidens sit at their looms. And here is where the knights keep their armor, and high up here is the tower where the princess lives." As she drew the lines of the rooms with her stick, she described them in such detail that I could see them rising before my eyes. The banner-hung hall, the great rotating spit, the trestle table, the tankards of mead, the troubadours with their guitars, the maidens clad in their clinging white homespun garments, the pages kneeling on embroidered cushions, the old women bustling about with the keys to closets hanging at their waists—I saw them all. Finally, we reached the tower room, where the princess sat looking out on the fair green meadows and lazily winding river. "And who is the princess?" I would ask. "You are," Gwladys would answer. "You have long golden hair down to your knees and deep-blue eyes, and the fairest white skin with pink cheeks. And you have a chaplet of wildflowers on your head and a silver kirtle around your waist."

"A kirtle?" I asked, bewildered.

"Overskirt," snapped Gwladys, annoyed at being interrupted.

"And who are you?" I demanded, already knowing the answer.

"A witch," said Gwladys, "a dreadful, terrible old witch with one tooth like a Chinese sword, eyes like burning coals and long black snakes for hair and fingernails three feet long with a different poison in each nail." I shuddered and was almost afraid to raise my eyes, because I knew that Gwladys was turning herself into the witch at that very moment. From being a meek, furtive little girl, she became a thing of terror and menace, a hideous crone full of hate and fury. No Electra or Medea was

A party in front of Minister Calhoun's house in the American legation. If I remember correctly, it is Henry Pu-yi scratching his head in the first row (at left).

A legation party.

Taken at the British legation.
Harrison Hatch (left) played Benjamin Franklin
to my Priscilla Alden.

The same party, but a bigger group—
also all legation children. My friend Anna is at left.

ever so terrible. My role as the peaches-and-cream princess was that of the fly caught in the spider's web. I had my beauty and my fine garments and eventually my prince (because Gwladys was fair-minded), but I certainly had to suffer for it. Up and down the stairs of the castle, running ever faster and faster, ducking behind a tapestry, crawling under a silken table cover, or even hanging from a battlement—it was to no avail. Gwladys always caught up with me. And each time my blood would run cold anew with the horror of my predicament. It was only toward the end of the afternoon, when teatime was approaching, that she would allow the prince finally to do her in. Her death agonies were hideous to behold and, in her last moments, a dreadful curse came to her snarling lips. Tears of fear and horror used to spring to my eyes, but I think now that I was really only paying tribute to a magnificent performance. No Bernhardt or Duse could have been more convincing.

When Amah called us for tea, Gwladys picked herself up calmly from the ground where she was playing her death scene and, smoothing down her dress and hair, became again a rather unattractive, dull-looking girl.

I could not come back to our own world so easily. It took a couple of cups of tea and a few sandwiches before I could look at her with equanimity. Our game varied according to the books that Gwladys was reading. But our roles were always essentially the same. I the vapid, timid goody, Gwladys the hideous, all-powerful incarnation of evil. With the other children I knew I played the games that children have always played. But hide and seek and spoon-and-egg race and pinning the tail on the donkey, under the supervision of a kindly governess, were pretty dull when compared to the breathtaking, mad afternoons with Gwladys. Even at that early age I found it more fun to be frightened than to be bored.

I had another friend who hardly knew of my existence. His name was Johnny Malone and he was a bugler in the United States Marines. He had curly black hair, blue eyes, long sweeping lashes, and rosy cheeks. When he stood up straight in the middle of the compound, blowing out a call on his shining bugle, his white belt drawn snappily tight around his slender waist, I thought he was the most beautiful thing I had ever seen. Because of him I learned every single bugle call—from reveille through mess call, sick call, stable call, inspection, right down to flag-down and taps. On the days that he was sounding flag-up, I used to stand in bed in my long nightgown, my hand raised to my forehead in a smart salute. "Johnny," I would whisper, "dear, beautiful Johnny!"

In the winter a large space in our compound was flooded to make an ice-skating rink. It had a corrugated iron roof, matting walls, and electric light for late-afternoon and evening skating. It was primarily for the men, but the officers and their families could use it on certain days when the band played. Often, there were hockey games between the different companies of Marines and sometimes between our Marines and the soldiers of other guards.

Johnny Malone was a magnificent skater, darting over the ice like a bird, taking the puck from one end of the rink to the other, dodging all interference from the opposing team. I would jump up and down screaming, "Go it, Johnny," at the top of my voice, my pigtails flying in the air.

One day, when the band was playing and I was skating crossed-hands with Father's orderly, Royce, we saw Johnny leaning nonchalantly against the railing. "How would you like to skate with Johnny Malone?" said Royce, his eyes twinkling. I almost slipped and fell. I gathered that Royce had an inkling of my feeling and I was overcome with embarrassment. But before I could answer, Royce raised his voice. "Johnny-boy," he called, "come on over and take the Major's little girl around the rink for a turn."

Johnny skated over in a slow, easy way. "Sure," he said, smiling, "it will be a pleasure."

Royce skated off and Johnny took my little fur paws in his

Coming home from a party in the Chinese City in a rickshaw, this is what I saw—a scene that has haunted me often since.

hands. In my excitement I began to skate out wildly. "Easy, now, easy," he said, "just listen to the music." It seemed impossible that I could really be going around the rink with my hero. I looked up at his long, sweeping lashes and thick, curly hair. What a beauty he was!

I drank my fill of that exquisite moment and then he looked down at me and caught my eye. "Having fun?" he asked, smiling. "I have a little sister in Boston just about your age." "Have you?" I murmured. And then, as we rounded the bend on our way back to Royce, I felt that I had to be more audacious and say something personal. "I love to hear you play the bugle," I bleated. "You are the best bugler in the whole band." "Thank you," he said, "I sure love to play it. You are a very nice little girl." I trembled all over at this compliment.

I never spoke to him again, but the day before we left Peking I went out into the compound and, hiding behind some large crates, I watched him as he stood by the flagpole. He had on his dark-blue tunic, light-blue trousers with the broad red stripe, and white belt with brass buckle. He was sounding stable call and, to this day, I cannot hear it or whistle it without thinking of him. Wherever you are, Johnny Malone, old and fat and beaten by life, perhaps, I will always remember you, standing like a young god with the shining golden bugle raised to your lips, sending out your clarion call for the drones of the world to get about their business.

Not all the children I played with lived in the Legation Quarter. The children of customs officials, missionaries, and business people lived in the Chinese City. I was having tea with a friend whose father was head of the Mission for the Blind and who lived in the Chinese City on the day that the Revolution broke out. I used to love to go there because the blind Chinese girls were so gentle and kind and I indulged my passion for storytelling with them. It was a great occasion for me to show off and I painted the world in glowing colors. They would sigh softly, as they made their lace or straw work, and would plead sweetly, "More, little girl, tell us more!" My friend who lived there was an amiable child, several years older than I, but she could only quote the Bible and parables while I boldly invented tales of demons and spirits and beautiful princesses.

Entranced by this form of autointoxication, on this particular day I lingered on until it was almost dusk and Amah came clucking impatiently. "Little Missy no can stay," she chided. "Must be home or Mistress get cross." We went out to our rickshaws waiting in the smelly hutung, which was walled by private houses on each side, some grand, some very poor.

As we came out we saw that something was amiss. "We must hurry," said my rickshaw boy, "there are bad men around, Little Girl. We must get back to the Legation Quarter."

We started off at a great pace and all seemed well until we turned into the Hata Mên. Shopkeepers were putting up their shutters and taking down their signs, and people were scurrying inside like leaves before the wind. The usually busy street was almost deserted. As we went along we began to see why. Down the middle of the road were tripods and hanging by their pigtails from these tripods were severed heads. Lying as if face down were bodies, their hands tied behind their backs. The heads themselves were what held my terrified eyes. The eyes were staring and great bloody cords hung from their necks. I could hear Amah screaming in English behind me, but I knew that it was no use to speak. My coolie was running as fast as he could and I was so frightened that I felt frozen as though in a nightmare.

At that moment there came toward us at a brisk trot down the middle of the street a little band of British soldiers. The sergeant in charge dashed up to me. "Are you the American commandant's little girl?" he panted. "Yes," I squeaked. "Thank God," he answered. "We have been looking for you." Then to his men, "This is the child. We will see her home." They formed a line on each side of my rickshaw and, crouching down in it, I could only see the red of their jackets and their nice, shining faces instead of those horrible heads.

When we got to our legation, there were sandbags across the entrance and Marines standing "at the ready." Some sandbags had to be moved to let us through. After thanking the British soldiers, Amah and I were deposited at our door. Mother embraced me hysterically and I clung to her, still too frightened to cry. Those dreadful heads haunted me for years.

Father was gone all night and then the next day a contingent from each legation paraded together in formation through the Chinese City. It was only little more than a decade after the Boxer Rebellion and no one wanted a repetition of *that*. Yüan Shih-k'ai was installed as president; little Pu-yi was relegated to the background (he later became an ardent Communist). Almost immediately pigtails started to disappear and the mandarins disposed of their outriders. Peking began to lose its feudal atmosphere and was never quite the same again.

Peking Diary

A tea party with Gwladys and my dog, Gyp

Author's note: I wrote this diary at age ten.

My name is Brooke Russell,

Names of my pets—"Gyp" a darling dog, all mine. Fido—a puppy half mine (the other half is Father's) Ginger—my pony.

Father, commanding officer American Legation Guard

Calhoun, minister

Williams, first secretary

Summerlin, 3rd secretary

Jan 1 1913 Went to Mme Pierrie's to a party. Was very late, and sat at a table all by myself but had a nice time afterwards.

Jan 3rd Went and saw the balley at the French Legation. Miss Benchell was the Rose Queen—Monsieur de Lucca a fly—Madame Beauvaux Queen of the fairy's, mother a daisy—Monsieur Gravé was a grasshopper.

Jan 5th Gwladys came to tea and I went to lunch with her. We played fairy stories. Counted my Christmas presents. Got 320.

Jan 6th Am learning how to skate with 2

feet. Used to do one. Gwladys came to tea and we played with paper dolls.

Am learning to skate awfully fast. Gwladys came to tea, and went home at 7. We played with Evie.* To-morrow is Evie's birthday.

Had music lesson. Skated—had only just got on the ice when I had to come off. The cook made a cake for Evie. Gwladys came. Gyp and Fido had cambric tea.

Saturday Got up at 8. Wrote poems until 11, then skated till 1 o'clock. Gwladys came to tea, began my novel, Beauty Blackwell. Poem enclosed "Bleat, Bleat, Bleat". Skated with Johnny Marlone,† Rain-water and Shay and Gwladys. She came to tea and we wrote stories.

Skated. had music lesson. Went to Lady Jordan's and was dressed as a rose. Had a lovely time. More than twenty-two children there.

Miss Isabelle Piry invited me to tea, but Gwladys was coming to tea. So I couldn't go. Mother was cross. I am reading the Swiss Family Robinson.

Went to Eileens house to tea. She leant me 2 books. The Fairy Rings, and the Magic Nuts. Had a nice time.

Went to the Fair at the Temple of Agriculture. Bought Rachel some toy birds and 2 little pots of flowers.

Love Rachel. Went to school and had to walk home because the mafoo hit my pony in the eye.

Went to Gwladys to tea. Mrs. Williams scolded me. I came home and cried, and burnt my novel. Alas!

*Evie was a life-sized wax doll with real hair.

†A young bugler and father's orderly.

Chinese New Year. Hocky game, between british sargents, and american sargents. We won. Saw Johnny Malone playing the Buggle. He looked beautiful.

Went to Monsier de Hoyer's balley. Oh it was just lovely, and they had a french comedy afterwards.

Father came to kiss me when I was asleep last night and Gyp bit him.

Gwladys came to tea. We wrote stories. Beauty Blackwell is a sad story. Saw Darlingo*

Went to Gwladys, had a nice time and a happy day.

Skated all morning. Saw Darlingo skating. Went to tea with Eileen and Edie. We made paper dolls.

The Empress Dowager died, I think that she was poisoned, although they say she had dropsy.

Fuzzy scratched Gyp's eyes. Oh I hate Fuzzy. She's a horrid mean cat. Oh I think he's going blind she scratched so.

Mother and Father quarelled at lunch, and then remained cross. So, I told Father to go over to the K.T. Club,† so as to see Mother. Father is like a snail without a shell without Mother.

Mother wants me to be in a Pantomine at the British Legation. I'm supposed to be a poor little girl, who a fairy makes into a princess.

Gwladys came to tea. We played in Mrs. Calhouns grape arbor. We were wild. Couldn't sleep.

*The bugler Johnny Malone.

†One of the young diplomats kept open house at cocktail time, and called it "the K.T. Club."

Chapter 8

"The Surprise"

There was the matter of my education, for naturally I had to be educated. We got off to a false start by engaging an English governess who had the incredible name of Miss Muffett. She was thin and long like a handkerchief soaked in cambric tea and, without knowing what it was she did to me, I yawned in her face, fell into a daydream when she talked to me, and could not look her in the eye. In other words, she bored me. She did not bore me half as much as she did my family. All conversation dragged at the luncheon table and nothing more interesting was said than "Well, Brooke, how did your lessons go today?" or "Are you quite sure you are comfortable in your room, Miss Muffett?" It was dull, dull, dull and we were only released when Miss Muffett would say, "Oh, dearie me, it's very late. I think that Brooke and I should be off." What we did together when we went off amounted to absolutely nothing. She taught me to sing a dreary song which started off "Underneath the gaslight's glitter stands a little flower girl. . . ." She also taught me the different ranks in the British aristocracy, as she knew her Debrett by heart. Otherwise, I can't remember a single thing that I learned from her.

I never knew what happened but one day Miss Muffett was gone. "Gone to look after some little English girls in Tientsin," said Mother, "and you are going to the British School. I want you to be with other children, you are too much alone." It was easier to study away from home, where there were so many things to distract me, and also I had the fun of riding to and from school every day.

There is one out of all my schooldays in Peking that I remember particularly. It was a very special day. I wrote it all down in my diary, because everything done that day had significance. I was eight at the time and we had been in Peking a year. This particular day, as soon as I woke up I jumped out of bed and ran to the window overlooking the compound, which was an austere place: a large dusty square, surrounded by high gray stone walls, at one end the officers' quarters and along the side

(previous page)
In Peking on the steps of Ambassador Calhoun's house. Mother is at left.

the barracks where the men lived. As Father was in command, we had the largest house, which boasted a small garden with a cherry tree in it—a grafted one with half-pink, half-white blossoms. On this morning, as I looked out the window, I was horrified to find that a strong sand-filled wind from the Gobi Desert hung like a thick curtain beyond the windowpane. I could just make out the train of camels being unloaded. The camels rested with their forelegs folded under them and turned their heads contemptuously as the coolies worked to relieve them of their burdens. I hated the camels. They came twice a month bringing supplies and they were very mean and sly— always trying to nip me as I passed. I was not interested in *them.*

The important thing this morning was the weather. Today was to be the day of a great surprise. But Father had said that if it rained the surprise could not happen. As I looked out (and just for luck stuck my tongue out at a camel whose beady eye caught mine), I wondered if sand was as bad as rain or would it be all right for the surprise.

I kissed the three dogs and five dolls good morning, because they were all still in my bed and half asleep, then rushed down the stairs. As I rounded the dining-room door, I tripped on my long nightgown and fell headlong at Father's feet.

"Whoa, there!" he said, laughing. "Are you racing for a train or training for a race?"

"Oh, Father," I said reproachfully as he pulled me to my feet. "Racing for a train" was one of the sayings he loved to repeat and, even at the age of eight, I thought it unworthy of him.

"No, Father," I said impatiently. "Is it a good day for . . . you know, the big surprise . . . is it?"

He put some jam on a piece of toast and popped it into my eagerly opened mouth. "I don't know," he said. "This wind is bad. But the surprise isn't going to happen until this afternoon and it may clear up by then."

I helped myself to a spoonful of jam, then wiped my hands on my nightie.

There is one out of all my schooldays in Peking that I remember particularly. It was a very special day. I wrote it all down in my diary, because everything done that day had significance.

"Is it a new doll," I asked, "or a new dog?"

"Oh, no," said Father, getting up from the table. "It's a sort of bird. Wait till you see it. And now be a good little girl and run along."

At that moment Amah came into the room and, after bowing to Father, took me firmly by the arm. "It's not nice, Little Missy, to run around in your nightgown," she said crossly, "and you will be late for school. Hully, hully." I went along, keeping pace with her tiny steps. She had "lotus bud" feet and swayed prettily as she walked. I had seen her feet once without her socks and had been haunted by the sight for days. In babyhood, the toes had been fastened to the heel so that the only way the foot could grow was up—to form a great high instep. Consequently, the foot itself was the size of a baby foot. In the little satin shoes with the red tassels, the feet looked very provocative peeping out from Amah's black silk trousers.

"Amah," I said while she was dressing me, "Father says that the surprise is a bird. I don't want a bird. I don't like things in cages. Besides, a bird isn't any fun!"

"Stand still, Little Missy," she said as she tied the bow on my hair. "If Master wants to give you a bird, I think you like." Which, of course, was true. If Father gave me something that *he* liked, I knew that I would like it, too. It must be a very unusual bird, though, because he knew how I felt about birds as pets.

After my hearty breakfast of cocoa, buttered toast, prunes, and two soft-boiled eggs, I went up to kiss Mother good morning. She was lying in bed propped against the pillows waiting for her breakfast. "Hold your shoulders back," she said as I came in. "Keep your chin up." Shoulders back momentarily and chin up, I marched over and gave her a kiss. She smelled deliciously of rice powder and oil of lilies of the valley.

"What's the surprise, Mother?" I asked as she straightened the riding cap on my head. "Is it a bird?"

She laughed. "Wait and see. Perhaps you won't even like it."

What a thought! A chill struck my heart. It *was* a bird, probably a poor little canary. As I walked slowly down the stairs I made up my mind that if it *was* a bird, I would take it out in its cage when *I* went walking, as the Chinese did, and that I would always keep it covered at night. Once I had heard a canary singing all night in a hotel in San Francisco. I was only five at the time. They told me that the bird sang because it was in a restaurant where the lights were left on and the poor

bird thought it was day, whereupon I cried and cried. It seemed so terribly sad that it should sing like that for people who did not love it. Ever since then I had refused to have a bird for a pet, even though in Peking there were fascinating ones of beautiful plumage and talkative habits.

Still depressed, I went out into the compound, where Mafoo was waiting for me with my little Mongolian horse, Ginger. Mafoo and I always spoke Pekingese, and he greeted me this morning with a grin. "You are going to have to gallop all the way," he said. "You are late."

"But I can't gallop," I said, "because of the dust; it will be bad for you." I had been told that the life of a rickshaw coolie running through the dust of Peking was only six years, and I loved Mafoo.

"Don't worry, Little Girl," he said, grinning broadly, "a Japanese friend of mine has given me a fine thing."

He took a gauze hospital mask out of his pocket and put it over his face. His merry slant eyes peering over the white gauze looked so strange and funny that I began to laugh. "All right," I said, "let's go." I jumped into the saddle and, flicking Ginger with my crop, dashed off at top speed, my pigtails

In order to go to school every day, I rode on Ginger through the Russian parade ground, and Mafoo would run alongside. Then he would come back for me after school.

flying straight out behind me and Mafoo running steadily at my side.

Out through the gate of the American legation and along the edge of the Russian parade ground we went till we came to the British legation. Across the compound was the odd-looking building which served as that school. It was really a bowling alley built as a recreation center for the British soldiers. Assembled in the little entrance room, formerly a lounge and meeting place, stood the heterogeneous group of American and British children, ranging in age from six to thirteen, who made up the school roster. They were the children of diplomats, officers, and customs officials and were a rather dull lot.

Our schoolmistress was a Scottish governess who, coming out to Peking with a family, had stayed on after the family had returned home. Looking back, I think that she must have been the victim of an unhappy love affair or other frustrating youthful experience. She certainly had no interest in us as children and had strange ideas of education.

I hung my cap and coat on the peg by the door and, hastily adjusting the pinafore ruffles over my shoulders, took my place beside my desk and started to chant with the others. Miss Leach gave me a severe glance and tapped her pointer impatiently.

> If I have faltered more or less
> In my great task of happiness;
> If I have moved among my race
> And shown no glorious morning face;
> If beams from happy human eyes
> Have moved me not; if morning skies,
> Books, and my food, and summer rain
> Knocked on my sullen heart in vain,—
> Lord, thy most pointed pleasure take,
> And stab my spirit broad awake;
> Or, Lord, if too obdurate I,
> Choose Thou, before that spirit die,
> A piercing pain, a killing sin,
> And to my dead heart run them in!

Our chanting stopped and we burst into one hearty verse of "God Save the King," then sat down stiffly in our seats. If we slumped in our seats, a board was fastened to our backs and that was most uncomfortable.

The first lesson was grammar and we got out the little paper boxes that we had made the week before. These boxes were crayoned in different colors and had written on them: "nouns," "prepositions," "adjectives," and "verbs." Our object was to copy the sentence Miss Leach wrote on the blackboard, then cut out the words with our blunt scissors and put them in the proper boxes. While we did this, Miss Leach resolutely read the Bible to herself. The sentence this morning was a long one: "A full, busy youth is your only prelude to a self-contained and independent age, and the muff inevitably develops into the bore." —Signed R. L. Stevenson.

Mother had a red fox muff, so I knew what that was. And I also had heard her call a person a bore but the rest of the sentence was beyond me. However, nothing daunted, I crayoned my words and threw them recklessly into the colored boxes.

At eleven o'clock we all went into the bowling-alley part of the building and had a cup of hot soup. As it was cold there, Miss Leach whistled "We'll Make the Keel Row," and we danced the Highland fling to warm up. Miss Leach danced, too, and grew very red in the face, whistling and dancing at the same time. I was quite good, so she put down two sticks to represent crossed swords and I jumped nimbly in and out of them. At last, panting and breathless, we returned to our desks.

We had our English history lesson next—all about King Alfred and pancakes, which made me think of a song of Father's. I raised my hand. "Yes, Brooke," said Miss Leach, brightening, "what is it?" We had been rather apathetic that morning and I suppose a glimmer of interest seemed like manna to her.

"Please, Miss Leach," I said, "my Father sings a song:

> Buckwheat cakes and pumpkin pie
> Made the British Redcoats fly!

What does it mean?"

"Ask your father," snapped Miss Leach, "and, Brooke, you are not paying attention today. I want you to stay after school for some special dictation."

The tears welled in my eyes. What an unfair thing! I *had* to be home for the surprise. I struggled through the morning, listless and inattentive, and had to have the board strapped to my back because of my bad posture. Once again the gross blindness and unkindness of the Grown-up world had been forced upon me and I resented it fiercely. Why couldn't Grown-ups mind their own business and let children mind theirs? I looked dully out the window. The wind had gone down and the pale sunlight of the April morning was coming through. It was going to be a nice day, after all, and I simply had to be there. Pounds, shillings, pence, and farthings—who cared whether one could divide, subtract, or add them—of what importance were they to anybody?

At last, the morning drew to a close. We stood up once more and this time we chanted:

> If I should die, think this of me,
> Here he lies where he longed to be;
> Home is the sailor, home from sea,
> And the hunter home from the hill.

What misanthropic thoughts possessed Miss Leach to have our childish voices bleating out this watered-down version of Stevenson I will never know, nor why we started and ended our school day with Stevenson.

We sang "God Save the King" again and scrambled for our coats. I was furtively reaching for my cap when I felt a strong hand on my shoulder. "You must stay, Brooke, and do your dictation. Sit down and get out your copybook."

The easy tears came to my eyes. "Oh, please, Miss Leach," I pleaded. "I am sorry if I was stupid, but please, may I do my dictation tomorrow instead of today?"

"Why?" she demanded, tapping her ruler against her desk.

"Because there is to be a special big surprise and Father wants me to be there." At this moment dear Mafoo put his head in the door. "Master said you were to come quickly, Little Girl. Why haven't you got your coat on?"

Miss Leach, who understood Chinese perfectly, glared at him but relented toward me. "All right, go," she said, "but tell your parents that you were rude and must stay tomorrow."

"Yes, Miss Leach. Thank you," I chirped happily. Tomorrow is always far off when one is eight.

Back I galloped, out the gate past the British guard, along the edge of the Russian parade ground, where the Cossacks seemed to be pushing something huge around, and back through the gate of our own legation, where the Marines smiled indulgently as I dashed through.

Mother and Father had finished lunch and Father had already gone out. So I had my lunch on a tray in my room, surrounded by my family of dolls and dogs. Amah came in as I was finishing, bringing my new tan coat and tan Scottish cap with her.

"Why do I have to put that on?" I asked. Amah and I spoke English because she, being from Shanghai, could not understand Pekingese.

"Because Mistress says so," said Amah smugly. "Many people are coming today." Then she took a new pongee dress with pale-blue smocking out of the closet.

"Oh, dearie me," I moaned (an expression left over from Miss Muffett), "do I have to be all dressed up?"

Along with members of various legations, my father, (front, second from left) in Peking with Yüan Shih-kai, first president of China (front, center)

"Yes," said Amah, laying the dress on the bed. "Many mandarins and princes and fine foreign ladies and gentlemen are coming. Kwai, kwai" ("quick, quick" in Pekingese). It was the only Pekingese she knew and I knew she said it to please me, because I loved to talk Chinese. So I allowed her to dress me, unplait and brush my hair so that it could hang shining down my back, and put my cap on at a rakish angle.

"Now Little Missy looks nice," she said, smiling. "Mistress is in the drawing room, waiting."

I trotted down to find Mother standing by the door. She was all dressed up in a new silk suit that Tailor had made for her. She had on a hat of cock feathers and a boa of cock feathers around her neck, and I thought she looked lovely. She took me by the hand and we hurried out and crossed from the Legation Compound, where we lived, to the legation itself. There, next to the legation gate and built high up over the wall which surrounded the compound, were wooden bleachers. As we approached, I saw that many people, both foreign and Chinese, were already seated.

Mother and I climbed up almost to the top, where some seats were being saved for us. Father was standing down by the gate with the first secretary of the legation, obviously waiting for someone. We waved to him. He was in full uniform, complete with sword, so he gave us only a snappy salute and smiled. Around us were the heads of foreign missions and the commandants of the guards: British, French, German, Russian, Italian, Japanese—all the top people in the Legation Quarter. The Chinese were mostly mandarins dressed in long silk robes and wearing small jeweled caps, their glossy pigtails braided into tassels ornamented with jade.

As I watched, more and more people poured through the legation gate. The foreigners came in rickshaws. In some instances the rickshaws had not only a man between the shafts but another man pushing for more speed. The Chinese, being mostly of high rank, came in their small closed carriages.

The carriages kept on careering through the gate until at last the man Father was waiting for arrived. It was Prince W.—who had been on the steamer with us coming up the Yangtze! When the four horses pulling his carriage were brought to an impatient standstill and his twelve noisy outriders lined up, he emerged slowly and sedately. He was a dignified man with a long, aristocratic beard and an elegant pigtail. His hands were in the sleeves of his robe as he bowed to Father, but his intelligent eyes were restlessly surveying the throng. Father, I could see, was addressing him in his best Mandarin. Then Father led him with great ceremony to a seat just in front of Mother and me, and next to the American minister.

I was glad that I had on my new coat and cap when the prince turned and smiled at me and said in coolie, because he knew I could not speak Mandarin, "Good day, Little Girl."

But now a noise arose. The great thing that the Cossacks had been uncovering that morning was being pushed out into the middle of the field. "What is it?" I asked Mother.

"It is an airplane," said Mother, "and it has been brought over from America with an American crew to fly it."

"But what is it going to do?" I demanded.

"We hope it is going to fly," answered Mother, looking at it through her opera glasses. "But of course we don't know. We have never seen one before."

I looked at it curiously. It had wings on the sides and a seat in the middle that a man wearing a cap and goggles was climbing into. Two other men were hanging on to something in front and were trying to spin it. I yawned. "I'm feeling teatime-ish," I said.

"Hush," said Mother, and Father, leaning back to look at me, said: "Brooke, what you are seeing today may very well change your whole life." It was not like Father to make such an exaggerated statement and so I became attentive.

The birdlike thing was moving. It had turned and gone back on its wheels to the far end of the Russian area. It stopped there for a moment, then with a great roar came toward us, faster and faster, gathering momentum as it came. The crowd watched in breathless silence. Was it going to bang into our wall? What was it going to do? Suddenly, like a great awkward bird, it began to rise higher and, wobbling from side to side, it passed slowly and unsteadily about fifty feet above our heads.

The crowd rose in silent amazement to watch it, and the Marines below let up shrill whistles. As we watched, it rose slowly over the walls of Peking and then circled back over the yellow-tile roofs of the Imperial City. From that distance it looked more like a bird than ever and I thought that, after all, the surprise really *was* a bird. The people in the stands began to cheer and whistle and stamp their feet.

Prince W. watched in serene silence and Father, turning to him, in his excitement spoke in English. "Excellency," he cried, "isn't it marvelous that the machine can really fly!" The prince smiled politely and answered in perfect English, "But surely, my dear Major, that can't surprise you. You invited me here to see it fly."

"That was the damnedest thing," said Father when we three were finishing our tea. "I simply can't imagine Prince W., who is such an intelligent man, not being excited at seeing a first flight."

"But, John," said Mother, "don't you realize that nothing surprises the Chinese? You invited him to see a flying machine, so he expected to see it fly. It would have excited him only if a machine designed to fly hadn't flown."

Father sighed. "I guess you are right, Mabel," he said. "But how can we ever understand them or they us?"

Chapter 9

Mabel and John

It was on my parents' tenth wedding anniversary that I began to be aware of them as individuals. Up to then I had thought of them as twin beings, who had complete control over me and played into each other's hands. Then suddenly on this day, through a crack in their armor as parents, I caught a glimpse of something different—John and Mabel.

We were having lunch—a very special lunch to celebrate the occasion. I was sitting between them, lost in a happy dream world of my own. Between luscious bites of roast venison (we ate a great deal of venison in Peking) and wild rice, I was going over in my mind's eye every detail of the wedding ten years before. Mother had recounted it to me many times, and I could see it as though I had been there. The white satin wedding dress, with real lace yoke and long real lace veil, the cream-colored "going away" suit trimmed in brown satin, the brown hat, which had two pheasant wings in front. I was imagining how such a costume would look on me, when I suddenly realized that the mood at the table had changed. When I had floated away, they were laughing and talking. Now there was a tension and a stillness. I looked up at No. 1 Boy to let him know that I appreciated the delicious luncheon, but his eyes were cast down, which was a habit of his when he wanted people to think he was not listening. Things must be serious. I turned to look at Mother. Her eyes looked very bright and her mouth was set.

"John," she was saying, "why are you so quiet today? I was just saying that I think we are really a most unusual couple, so much happier than most. And I think it is because in all our life together I have gone out of my way not to do anything that would annoy or upset you." Father went on eating quietly. "Have I ever annoyed you? Have I ever done anything you didn't like? Have I?" she demanded, looking at him searchingly and her voice rising. "For heaven's sake, stop eating and answer me."

Father looked up, his usually happy face a little sad and stern. Mother and I waited for his reply but he remained silent. Mother pushed her chair back and threw her napkin onto the table.

"How can you behave like this?" she cried. "Don't you love me at all? I left Papa's house, and have followed you all over the world, making your life mine, and now on our wedding anniversary you turn on me. You obviously don't love me."

"I *do* love you," said Father seriously, looking across at her. "But I *have* been cross and annoyed sometimes."

Mother burst into a flood of tears and jumped up. "How can you say such a thing?" she sobbed. "And in front of Brooke, when I have thought of nothing but you in ten years. I'm through with you, you have no heart!" She stamped her foot and her eyes flashed, and then she ran out of the room.

I had lost my appetite and pushed my plate from me. My world was in jeopardy and I could not stay silent to see it crumble. "Aren't you going after her, Father?" I asked anxiously.

He looked at his watch, and then he, too, jumped up. "I'm late," he said, "I must go back to the office," and hurried out. At the door, he looked back and smiled at me. "Don't worry, Brooke," he said. "Mother just doesn't feel very well today, she will be all right later."

I knew that he had smiled only with his mouth, not his eyes. Even at nine I was beginning to learn the quality of a smile. The family had left the table in such a hurry that dessert had not been served. So now No. 1 Boy put before me a floating island garnished down its side with maraschino cherries.

"No, Number One," I said, "I'm not hungry."

"Little Girl likes this very much," he said coaxingly.

I shook my head. I was very near to tears. "No, not today," and I left the table.

I trudged upstairs and listened outside Mother's door. A muffled sob came from within. I tried to turn the knob, but the door was locked. I returned disconsolate to my room. It was raining, and so I could not play outside. The five dolls—Geraldine, Evie, Harry, Priscilla, and Rachel—were in my room seated on the little chairs around their own table. They were waiting for me to do something to amuse them, and their eyes looked at me

Mother and Father quarreled at lunch, and then remained cross. So, I told Father to go over to the K. T. Club, so as to see Mother. Father is like a snail without a shell without Mother.
—from my Peking diary

inquiringly. "Not now," I said, rather annoyed, "you will have to wait until it's teatime."

I curled up on the sofa by the window and looked out at the rain pelting the compound. Only an occasional Marine wrapped in a black rubber poncho was to be seen. The three dogs jumped up and sat beside me. Gyp licked a tear which had trickled down my cheek. Amah came bustling in with a pile of my underclothes and began putting them away in the bureau drawers. By the anxious glances she gave me, I could see that she already had had the news through No. 1.

"Why doesn't Little Missy play with her dolls?" she asked.

"I don't want to," I said, looking out at the rain.

"Well," said Amah, "Tailor give me many nice pieces, satin and silk. Why not make a pretty dress for Rachel, Chinese fashion dress?" (Rachel was the Chinese doll.)

I shook my head. "No, Amah," I said, "I don't want to do anything."

Amah bustled around the room a few minutes more, then, seeing that I was not to be tempted, went out. No. 3 Boy came in with a scuttle of coal to put in the stove. We had no central heating, and stoves and fireplaces were our only form of heat. The halls were freezing in the winter, as there were no stoves in them, and we often caught cold going from one hot room through the icy halls to another hot room. By the way No. 3 looked at me, I realized that even *he* knew of the disaster. So when he left I slipped away to my favorite refuge. It was the closet where Amah kept Mother's evening dresses. Once there in the inky darkness, with the door closed, I felt safe. Normally I was afraid of the dark, but this was a darkness of my own creating. I knew that the world was light outside, and so I had no fear. What I loved was the swish of the dresses against my face. I sat down in the very middle of the rather shallow closet so that they descended in a cascade on me from all sides. Sequin-spangled tulle, satin, lace, stiff velvet, and soft velvet, all smelling faintly of oil of lilies of the valley. It was a remote and sensuous retreat.

I reveled in both my aloneness and the tangible feeling of beauty about me. I sat there for a long time, and as the air was stuffy, I suppose I dozed. I thought, of course, that no one knew where I was. But naturally a child who is supervised as I was had no real hiding place. In fact, Mother told me that she and Amah always knew when I went there.

This day, when I awoke, I heard sounds coming from Mother's room. Mother and Amah were talking, and Amah was making consoling noises as she hurried about. Evidently Mother was dressing to go out. She was also telling Amah what had happened at lunch. Finally, I heard the door close and Mother go downstairs. I came out and went into Mother's room. Amah was straightening the toilet articles on the dressing table, and smiled at me cheerfully.

"Where has Mistress gone?" I asked.

"Mistress gone to cocktail party," answered Amah.

I remembered that it was the day the American Bachelors had their cocktail party. They gave one every two weeks. The people invited were called "members" and they had long red tickets with K.T. printed on them, which entitled them to come whenever they felt like it. That Mother would want to go there on a day when she had shaken my whole world seemed unbelievable to me. "You sure, Amah?" I inquired.

"Oh, yes, velly sure," answered Amah, smiling. "Mistress take ticket. Headache all gone. Going to have a little fun."

I went in bewildered silence to my room. The Grown-up world was a continuing puzzle to me. The dolls were still at their table, but No. 3 had set it for tea. They had their own little cups and saucers with tiny roses on them, and there was a big one for me. In the middle of the table there was a plate of watercress sandwiches. I drank my tea moodily and only addressed an occasional remark to the dolls. They got very sad if no one talked to them, but only politeness kept me going that afternoon. My thoughts were not with them because my ear was cocked for the sound of the front door which would signal Father's return. I knew he would be sad. At last I heard it, and started running down the front stairs, reaching him just as he closed the door.

"Oh, Father," I cried, "I'm so glad you are home. I've been so lonely without you!"

He picked me up in his arms and swung me in the air, then laughed as he put me down. "Where is Mother?" he asked.

"Gone to the K.T. Club," I said solemnly.

"Oh," said Father, and as No. 1 Boy approached from the nether regions, he added, "Bring me a whiskey and soda in my study, please."

"May I come too?" I asked, hanging on to his hand.

He gave my hand a squeeze. "Of course," he said.

We went into the little back room that was his study. It was hideously furnished by the government in green velvet and imitation mahogany and Father had not allowed Mother to change it. She had put her touch on the other rooms, making them gay and cheerful with apricot linen and blue coolie-cloth slipcovers. But I imagine that even in China, with a good exchange of silver dollars, she must have spent quite a lot, and we were far from being rich.

The little study looked very stark, but it suited our mood. Father sat down in the Morris chair by the fireplace and I climbed onto his lap. "Now," I said, when my head was safely on his shoulder and his arm was around me, "sing."

Father waited until No. 1 had put the drink on the table beside him and had retreated. He had no voice and very little idea of a tune, but the songs he sang were fascinating to me. "A long time ago, boys, an Irishman named Dougherty," "One dark night on Lac St. Pierre the wind she blow, blow, blow . . .," "Alouette," "No, I will never marry anyone but Alvin Barry" (this was a sort of opera, and Father took several parts), "Chicken in the breadpie picking up dough," "It was indeedo a Norwich Torpedo." These were all old favorites, but today he sang a song he had never sung before: "My name, it is Jack Hall, Jack Hall, and I wear a chain and ball, chain and ball." It was a fearful song, and Father sang it with a sort of croak. It ended up with "Damn your eyes."

I shuddered and clung to him more closely. "Father," I said, "I never heard you sing that before, sing it again." But Father took a sip of his drink and shook his head. "No, Little Woman," he said, "I won't sing that anymore. It's not really a song for little girls."

"Well, then, let's both sing the Marines' Hymn," I suggested.

We had just started our rendition when we heard the front door close. Mother was home! We raised our voices a little, but she went straight upstairs and banged the door. We finished the Marines' Hymn and sang "Eternal Father, Strong to Save." Then Father put me down and got up.

"I'm going upstairs," he said.

I did not answer; there was nothing to say. But my heart was beating fast. Would Mother be good? I heard him running up the stairs two at a time, which was his habit. Then overhead I heard him rattling the handle of Mother's door, then silence. I crept upstairs, and as I passed Father's room I saw the red light of his cigar where he sat in the dark. The bed was turned down in my room, and the dolls were in a row at the foot. The dogs were lying asleep before the stove, and looked up lazily as I came in. All seemed calm and serene but, of course, I knew it was not.

I tiptoed through the back hall to the door of Mother's room that opened there. It was locked, and I began tapping, at first softly, then louder and louder. "Mother," I called, "Mother, please come out!" There was no answer, but I heard Mother moving about. "Please, please, Mother," I cried, "please come out. I want to say something to you!"

The anguish in my voice must have penetrated to her because she opened the door and let me in. She looked very upset and unhappy, and I knew that my chance had come! I had to plead Father's cause. "Oh, Mother," I implored, "do speak to Father. Without you he is like a snail without a shell. And he sang such

Mother on the stoop in front of our house, Peking

a terrible song to me today. He just isn't like himself without you. Mother, please, Mother dear!"

Mother began to laugh and cry at the same time. And, with me trotting behind her, she went over and unlocked the other door. "John," she called softly. But she didn't need to call because he was right there at the door.

"Darling," he said, putting his arms around her, "I'm so sorry."

"It was all my fault," murmured Mother as she kissed him. "You never have been annoyed or upset, have you?"

Father's "No" was so low that I could hardly hear it. It almost sounded like "Jack Hall." Then they turned and, bending down, both kissed me. I was wonderfully happy. "Now," I said to them, "I think I will go and put the dolls to bed properly."

About this time there was another episode which again made me see my parents as Mabel and John. At tea one day there was a strange *Alice in Wonderland* conversation which made no sense to me, though it seemed to mean something to them. No. 2 Boy came in to deliver a package to Mother as we sat around the tea table. She glanced at it and then put it aside. It seemed strange to me not to open a mysterious package at once, and my curiosity was aroused.

"What is it?" I asked. "Is it a present?" Mother nodded absently and I decided to push the matter.

"Then do open it, Mother," I pleaded. "Let's see what it is."

Father, who was lighting his cigar, became interested too. "Yes, Mabel," he said, "Little Woman and I are both curious. Open it." But Mother didn't seem to want to.

"Oh, it's probably a cumshaw from some shop," she said. Cumshaws were gifts of material, furs, jewelry, anything that the various merchants who came to our house in the morning cared to give. I sensed a change in atmosphere—something was meant that was not being said. I could not imagine why, but it obviously had to do with the package.

"Let's see what it is," said Father, in a rather gruff way, and Mother put on her "pretending" manner and slowly opened the package. What she saw made her laugh uproariously, although it didn't seem at all funny to me. It was a pretty white brocade purse with Mother's initials, M.H.R., in jade. What was making Mother laugh, however, was the card. She waved it over her head and laughed and laughed.

"It's from Morris," she said, her voice positively choked with laughter. I knew Morris was an officer under Father's command, a very nice man, and I could not imagine what was so funny.

Mother handed the card to Father. "To Mabel, ma belle," he read solemnly. "Toujours à toi, Morris." "What rot," and he gave the card back to Mother.

"He's rather a dear," said Mother, wiping the corners of her eyes with the tea napkin.

Father settled back in his chair. He seemed relieved. "He's rather an ass," he said.

"Why do you say that?" demanded Mother, nibbling on a cucumber sandwich. "I thought you said he was a good officer."

"Oh, well," said Father grudgingly, "a pretty good officer, but these European mannerisms of his make him a laughingstock among the Americans and British."

"Really," said Mother, smiling. She seemed very happy. "Well, he can't help it. He went to school in France and *I* think his manners are charming."

Father looked at the nice firm ash on his cigar (which I had learned was the test of a good cigar). "Any American who goes around kissing hands and talking French is an ass," he said, and then, looking at Mother, "Some of his fellow officers resent having him constantly pawing their wives' hands and kissing them."

"How provincial!" exclaimed Mother. "To resent Morris is almost like resenting a Frenchman's kissing the hand."

Father looked into the fire and said nothing. Mother looked at him rather anxiously, I thought. "Don't you agree?"

"Agree to what?" said Father, still looking into the fire.

"Why," said Mother, stirring her tea rapidly, "to the fact that it would be absurd to resent a European's kissing one's hand."

Father looked thoughtfully down at the end of his cigar. "Some Americans don't like the Europeans either," he said.

Mother put down her cup. "Well, that's ridiculous. It's uncivilized. We have to respect each other's customs."

"That's all very well," said Father. "I am only saying that some American men don't like to have these foreigners hanging on to their wives' hands and kissing them. One thing leads to another," he concluded cryptically.

"What do you mean, Father?" I asked. "Do you mean that if Monsieur—" Mother interrupted me. "Keep quiet, Brooke, your father and I are talking." Then she turned to Father. "I didn't know you felt this way, John," she said softly.

Father looked at her. "I am not talking about myself," he said. "I know you would never have your head turned by these ridiculous 'je ne sais quoi' young men. I am thinking how upset some of the officers get when their wives fall for all this folderol. Of course," he continued, smiling at Mother, "I am lucky. I know that you take all their antics for what they are worth and that you are my darling Mabel, and that you love me, and I love you."

Mother caught his hand. "How good you are," she murmured.

Father kissed her hand.

"You are behaving just like a Frenchman, Father," I cried. "I thought you didn't like hand-kissing."

Father kissed Mother's hand again. "Well, you see, Brooke, *your* mother is my wife, and that makes all the difference."

Amah came for me then, and I went off to have my supper. What a funny afternoon it had been.

When my parents began to emerge as Mabel and John, the knowledge came to me that we were not really a trinity. There were Mabel and John, and there was Brooke. I knew that they loved me, but I knew that I came second in both their hearts.

Mother loved Father, and she loved me, but she also had myri-
ad beaux and friends. In Father's life of the heart there was only
Mother and me. She was the all-consuming passion of his life.

Years later, when as a Grown-up I sat holding Father's hand
as he was dying, he suddenly opened his eyes and smiled and,
leaning close, I heard him whisper, "Brooke." I kissed him and
said, "Yes, Father darling, I won't forget," because that whispered
"Brooke" meant "Brooke, look after Mother." He would never
have allowed himself to die if there had been no one to look after
Mother.

Chapter 10

The Temple
of One Hundred
Courtyards

The climate of Peking is most uneven, freezing cold in winter, boiling hot in summer. So it was the custom for the foreigners to send their wives and children to a cooler place during the hot months. Pei Ta Ho, by the sea, was the most popular, a sort of little Deauville, filled with Western-style villas, bordering a broad beach. Here the legations made their summer capital (the men came up for weekends), and the round of entertaining, though less formal, continued almost at the same tempo as in Peking. We spent our first summer there, but after a second winter in Peking, Mother had other ideas. She broached the subject at cocktail time one day.

"I don't want to go to Pei Ta Ho this summer," she said. "It was much too gay last year and Peking has been terribly hectic this winter. Do you realize, John, that we have been out thirty-six nights in a row?"

"Do I!" groaned Father. "I'm absolutely all in."

"It's hell," said Mother, sipping her sherry.

I looked at them, bewildered. "Don't you like going out?" I asked. Every night when they came to kiss me good night they were always in a hurry to get to their party and seemed brimming over with excitement. It was an era of fancy-dress parties and Mother was constantly planning new and prettier costumes. Father usually went as a chef or Pierrot or just in a domino, but Mother had Tailor working night and day turning her into a Columbine, a Madame de Pompadour, a Reynolds painting, and once, when she danced the cakewalk with Willard Straight, into a black-faced mammy. Sometimes they had private theatricals. Mother had played Lady Bracknell in *The Importance of Being Earnest*, she had danced as a comet in a Ballet of the Stars that Signor di Lucca of the Italian legation directed, and appeared as a bird in long green feathers in a production of *Chantecler* at the French legation. I went to several of the rehearsals, and seeing Mother laughing, surrounded by Messieurs de Cartier and Pelakin and Maltzan and Max Müller and Casenave, I could hardly believe that she was not having fun.

(previous page)
Out in the Western Hills having a picnic. Mother and I made a new friend during our little trip.

"Don't you really *like* it?" I repeated, wolfing down a glacéed nut.

"Not really, it's just something we have to do." As she said it, No.1 Boy came in with the chit book.

Mother took the note out of the book. "It's an invitation from the Picots," she said to Father, "for next Thursday, and I see that they are sending chits to Summerlin and Lady ffrench and Brambila and de Cartier and the Calhouns. It looks like a good party and we happen to be free."

"It looks like some good bridge," said Father. "I think it would be fine."

Pei Ta Ho: our first summer home on the ocean outside Peking

Mother signed her acceptance in the chit book and No. 1 Boy hurried away with it.

"Well, there go ten days without a stop," said Mother. "I really must have a rest, John."

"Of course you must," said Father. "How about taking a courtyard in one of the temples in the Western Hills for the summer? It is only sixteen miles from Peking but much cooler and I could come up every weekend." As Mother looked at him, he added, "Of course, you would have a Marine guard and would be perfectly safe and, just to make you more comfortable, one of the Chinese-language officers could be there."

Mother sighed. "It sounds like heaven," she said. "Peking really has been too much for me this winter."

And so we ended up in July in the Temple of One Hundred Courtyards in the Western Hills. It was not one of the most beautiful temples and its situation, low down in the hills, was not the prettiest, but it was in desperate need of money, being one of the largest.

The fact that we wanted five or six courtyards was a bonanza to them. The government paid the rent and I suppose it was

A picnic in the Western Hills

small, but we might have been maharajas by the way we were received. All the priests were out to greet us as we arrived at the main gate, having ridden up on donkeys from the railroad station. The priests were dressed in black and bowed very low and were very solemn. The head priest led Mother and me and Mr. Holcomb, the Chinese-language officer, to our courtyards, where everything was in readiness. The servants had come out earlier to put up our camp beds and to make cooking arrangements. And the Marines had rigged up a shower, which consisted of a perforated gasoline can that, when one pulled a string, fell over on its side and spilled the water.

"Divine," said Mother. "Just perfect." Mr. Holcomb translated to the head priest, who wished us health and happiness and disappeared into his own courtyard.

It was a strange, tumbledown place in great disrepair. The gardens behind our courtyards were completely neglected, and in the courtyards themselves great weeds were growing rampant between the stones. But the air was clear and fresh and free of dust, and the nights were deliciously cool.

Amah slept in the room with me and I was very glad because at night one could hear the wild dogs, or "whonks," howling outside. Often in the morning a hen or two which had strayed outside the coop would be devoured, leaving only a few feathers to tell the tale. These wild dogs could leap very high walls, and I have often wondered since if they were not really wolves. My own little dogs, Gyp, Lulu, and Baby, crept close to me and trembled when they heard the savage howls and snarls outside.

In the daytime, though, all was calm and peaceful. The Marines, under Mother's eye, started cleaning up the courtyards and gardens of our domain. This had once been a very rich temple, and as we cleared we found little bridges and pools and bits of statuary. In the evening the head priest would often come and talk to Mr. Holcomb and seemed delighted with the improvements being made. Now and then I wandered into the parts of the temple that were open to the public. I loved the scent of the joss sticks and the cool, dark interiors. Some of the Buddhas were still shining and bright and others were darkened from years of smoking incense. But the priests were dedicated and diligent, and all altars had flowers on them and often cakes that the village people had brought and little fluttering prayer papers. The priests knelt before the altars, their faces rapt and remote. I would watch and wonder if Buddha someday would wink an eye or smile.

The activity of the Marines irritated No. 1 Boy, who felt that his position as head of the household was being usurped. He distinctly felt a loss of face and would only bow distantly and pretend not to understand English when Sowatki, our head orderly, tried to joke with him. I saw his displeasure and it upset me. I was happy in the temple and wanted everyone else to be happy. One day I caught him as he moved in his dignified way, carrying the tea tray from our courtyard to the kitchen courtyard. I followed him into the pantry end of the kitchen.

"Number One," I said in Pekingese, "what is wrong? Don't you like the temple?"

He shrugged his shoulders. "It's a very poor temple, and very inconvenient. I must share my pantry with Cook and make-learn cook, and I have no place to put my things or keep my accounts."

I sat down on the floor and looked up at him, and he bent down and gave me a sugared walnut from a jar on the shelf.

"Is not an honorable thing for me to be cramped like this," he continued. "I am sorry, Little Girl, but until I came to your honorable parents I had only worked as Number One for the heads of legations. Now I come to a simple major, an honorable man but only a soldier, not a diplomat. Also I do not get the squeeze to which I had become accustomed. My position is not what it was."

"Oh dear," I said, crunching my walnut in my teeth, "please, Number One, you won't leave us, will you?"

I loved No. 1 because he never forgot my dolls' or dogs' birthdays, and because of his influence over Cook, my life was a series of gastronomical treats.

"Please don't leave us," I pleaded. "Couldn't something be done to make you more comfortable here?"

He sat down on a stool opposite me. "You are a nice little girl," he said, "and I like your honorable parents. I am happy in the household and happy in Peking, even though the squeeze is small."

"But here," I persisted. "What about here? Couldn't we make you like it here?"

He looked very thoughtful and then spoke slowly. "Yes," he said, "things could be better. I want the big room in the next courtyard."

"But there's a Buddha there," I protested. "I saw some priests in there just this morning."

No. 1 got up and started to move briskly about, indicating that our interview was ended. "You asked me, Little Girl, and I told you. If I have that room I stay."

I was dumbfounded, but Cook came in and I knew that we could not talk before him, so I left.

That evening after dinner Mother and I were sitting in the garden. I had been playing with a family of hedgehogs that lived under a pine tree and Mother was reading Pierre Loti. I went over and sat on the ground at her feet. She was engrossed in her book and glanced down at me impatiently. "Why are you staring at me like that?" she demanded.

"I'm worried," I said.

"Worried?" Mother laughed a rather high laugh. "What on earth have *you* got to be worried about?"

"Number One Boy isn't happy here," I said. "He wants to leave us, and that worries me."

Mother quickly put aside her book. "Haven't I told you not to gossip with the servants?" she said. "I think it is a great mistake that you ever learned Chinese. All you use it for is backstairs gossip. Number One Boy is devoted to us."

"No, he isn't," I said, plucking at a piece of grass. When I saw Mother's shocked face I hastily amended my remark. "I mean, he does like us and all that, even though he doesn't get much squeeze with us."

Mother snorted. "More than we can afford," she said. But I hurried along.

"He likes us and wants to stay with us but he can't do his work in his present quarters. He wants more space. He wants the big room in the courtyard next to the kitchen."

Mother lit a cigarette. "But that's impossible. That belongs to the temple and there is a Buddha there. He must be crazy." She said it firmly, but I could see that she was worried, too. Our No. 1 Boy was really the best in Peking. Everyone wanted him, but in some miraculous way we had been able to hold on to him. To lose him would be a terrible loss of face for us.

"He has gotten above himself," she said, but I knew that in saying this she was whistling in the dark. "We'd better have this out right now."

She clapped her hands and when Amah appeared she asked her to tell No. 1 Boy to come at once. I sat in uneasy silence while we waited. What a hornets' nest I had stirred up now! I wanted to keep No. 1 Boy, but I also did not want Mother or the head priest to be cross. It was one of my first lessons in how disastrous it is to try to make people happy; much easier to go one's own way and not bother.

In his usual slow, dignified way No. 1 Boy came into the garden. "Missy want to speak to Boy?" he said in pidgin English.

"Yes," said Mother impatiently. "Why you tell Little Missy you no happy? Little Missy say you want more pantry, but no can do."

He bowed low. "No can work good fashion in small place," he said. "Likee velly much have big place. Me likee velly much have big room next courtyard."

"But you know you can't have that room," snapped Mother. "Buddha is there."

Now and then I wandered into the parts of the temple that were open to the public. I loved the scent of the joss sticks and the cool, dark interiors. Some of the Buddhas were still shining and bright and others were darkened from years of smoking incense.

With coolies and an orderly out in the country. I have my topee on.

A tower in the Western Hills near our temple

*A priest and attendants beginning a service at
the Temple of One Hundred Courtyards*

The pure marble Summer Palace outside Peking

"Allee samee, think can do," said No. 1 Boy again.

"Well," said Mother, lapsing into English, "if you think that you can do it, go ask the head priest. Tell him you want it but I don't, and then come back and tell me what he says."

"Velly good, Missy," said No. 1 and walked quietly away.

"It's all too absurd," said Mother, "but I really should hate to lose him. He's the best boy in Peking."

The next morning when we came out after breakfast, we saw that all was bustle in the kitchen courtyard. Coolies were moving chests and iceboxes and boxes filled with china, and No. 1 was standing in the center directing operations.

"What on earth is going on?" said Mother to Sowatki.

"I don't know, ma'am," he answered, "but it seems like they are moving things out of the kitchen into the next courtyard. That Number One Boy was in there and they threw that giant, big old god out on his head."

Mother let out a screech of horror. "The infidel, the beast!" she cried. "Go get Number One Boy and tell him to come to me at once, will you please, Sowatki?"

Sowatki, nothing loath to give No. 1 an order, hurried away, and Mother, who was dressed in a divided skirt for our morning donkey ride, beat her crop along her side and bit her lip. I could see that she was furious.

No. 1 came toward us at a ceremonial pace and bowed low before Mother. "Missy want to see Boy?" he said innocently.

"I certainly do!" exclaimed Mother. "Number One, what have you done? This is not our house, but a temple. It belongs to Buddha and the priests. I expressly told you not to take that room."

No. 1 smiled. "Everything allee right, Missy. I speakee priest. He say okay."

"Okay?" repeated Mother, dazed. "What do you mean, okay? Just what did you say to him?"

"I say rich American velly sad no have place for icebox, no have place for china and glass. Rich American no likee, perhaps no stay. Must have more room to make comfortable. So priest say, 'What they want?'"

"Oh, no!" said Mother, horrified. "And what did he say?"

"He say velly serious, must go talk to Buddha. So he go in and talk to Buddha. Stay long time, maybe an hour. Burn joss stick, say singsong, then he come out and he say, 'Allee right, Buddha go away, icebox come in.'"

"Number One, are you telling me the truth?" asked Mother, looking him in the eye.

No. 1 never flinched. "Yes, Missy. Priest tell me he speak to Buddha, rich American want this room and pay poor priest good money to help temple. Room belongs to Lord Buddha. What shall poor priest do? Priest say he pray long time, burn many joss sticks, say many singsongs, then Buddha, he speak."

No. 1 smiled. "Buddha he tell priest beat the gong, whiff, whiff, inside of Buddha go away, allee samee chair or table. Rich American can put icebox. By and by, rich American go away. Priest put Buddha back, all priests come say singsong, beat gong, whiff, whiff, inside Buddha come back. Allee samee, got fine Buddha again."

"Are you happy now, Number One?" said Mother.

"Velly happy, Missy," murmured No. 1. "Priest good man, temple velly nice."

Mother sighed and turned to me. "Let's go for our ride," she said. As we rode out of the courtyard on our donkeys I looked back and saw Buddha standing in a corner surrounded by packing cases. Did I imagine it or was he smiling?

Chapter 11

The Miracle

We had a very happy summer; the serenity and beauty of the hills and the temples had an effect on us all. The noise and dust of Peking seemed far away. I could have stayed there forever, but Mother—though she loved it too, and though Messieurs Casenave, Pelakin, di Lucca, etc., came out from time to time (to my disgust and annoyance, as they upset our routine completely)—became restive. After a certain period she began to talk about Tailor and the clothes she needed and how lonely Father was and how selfish we were to stay on. I knew the signs. We would leave the dear temple soon. So I was not surprised when we began packing and the "dorritty wagon" appeared.

The dorritty wagon was a high wagon with a rumble for luggage and was drawn by four mules. (It was really for the officers, to be used on expeditions.) It was pretty rough to ride in because the wheels had no tires and the Chinese roads, being built below the villages, were always deep, muddy ruts. But the mules were strong and brisk, the Marine driver cheerful, and the air bracing. We completed the journey without incident and arrived to find Father waiting on the steps. "Welcome back to Peking!" he cried, as though we had been away for years.

We had been back in Peking only about six weeks when a blow fell. A friend of Father's wrote from headquarters, saying that we would soon be leaving.

"I hope not until after the cotillion that de Cartier is giving," said Mother.

"I hope not until we have finished that special indoctrination course," said Father.

And I, the Little Bear, said, "I hope not until after my birthday."

It seemed incredible to me that we would leave Peking and I wondered what I could do to prevent it. I sought out No. 1 Boy in his cubbyhole next to the pantry, where he was busy adding up his accounts.

"Squeeze very poor this month," he said, looking up gloomily with his abacus in his hand.

(previous page)
First day out after arrival in Peking—on my donkey

I hated to see him downcast. "Can't you buy more wine?" I asked.

He shook his head. "Your honorable father said there was too much wine last month."

"What about cumshaws?" I said. Even I got cumshaws from people Mother dealt with.

No. 1 smiled sardonically. "Cumshaws are not like squeeze," he said. "I give all my cumshaws to my honorable father-in-law for his shop in the Hata Mên."

I could see that he was desperate, and I doubted whether the time was ripe to consult him about my own troubles. He took his teapot out of the padded case that kept it warm and poured himself a fresh cup. I looked up at the shelf over his head. His eyes followed my eyes. "Honorable Mistress said you were not to have any more sugar walnuts," he said, "so do not tell her that I give them to you." He handed me a handful, freshly made and still warm.

"Umm," I said, "Cook is wonderful."

He shrugged his shoulders. "A pretty good cook," he said, "but an inferior man, not very high-class." He took a sip of his tea and I munched on my nuts. It was a moment of peace and understanding; I decided to broach my subject.

"Number One," I said, "we may be going away."

He nodded gravely. "I know, that's why my squeeze is so important just now."

"But, Number One," I expostulated, "how could you know? I just heard Father talking."

He smiled condescendingly. "It is Number One's business to know everything that happens in the house. You think I just sit here?" He took a sip of tea and laughed. "Oh, Little Girl, you are only a very small girl."

I bridled. "Well, I know things, too," I said. "I know that Number Two Cook is getting almost as much squeeze as Cook, and that Little Boy, who is supposed to walk the dogs when I am at school, really ties them to a tree and watches the Marines playing baseball."

It seemed incredible to me that we would leave Peking and I wondered what I could do to prevent it.

Before replying, No. 1 put his teapot back in its case; then he spoke. "Little Girl," he said, "you came here to my office to tell me something. What is it?"

I sat cross-legged on the floor in front of him and looked up into his round, kind face. "I don't want to leave Peking," I said. "I don't want to leave you and Amah and Mafoo, my horse, and my dogs. I want to stay, Number One. We *must* stay here. What can we do?"

He shook his head sadly. "Nothing," he said. "There is nothing that you and I can do, Little Girl. If your honorable father gets orders, he must go."

"Well, there must be *something*," I said.

At this moment No. 2 Boy came in, and bowed low to No. 1. "Honorable Number One," he said, "an old priest from the temple in the Western Hills is here and wants to see Mistress. He has brought a present for her."

"Tell him I am coming," said No. 1 imperiously as he rose from his chair.

I scrambled to my feet. "Wait a minute, Number One," I said, "I have an idea."

He turned and looked at me. "Quick, Little Girl," he said, "I do not like to keep venerable priest waiting."

"It's about the priest," I said. "Don't you think he could help us? He is a very good and venerable man. You remember last summer how Buddha spoke to him. Well, if Buddha speaks to him, *he* can speak to Buddha. Why can't he ask Buddha to let us stay?"

No. 1 looked shocked, although I knew, and he knew that I knew, that he was not a very religious man.

"No, no," he said impatiently. "You can't do that. Mistress would not like it."

I caught the edge of his silk jacket. "Please, Number One," I begged. "Let me speak to the venerable priest. You can tell Amah to let Mother know that he is downstairs. That will give me time to talk to him, because Mother is not dressed yet."

He looked down into my pleading face and relented. "All right, Little Girl," he said. "You go and see the priest and I will send Number Two to tell Amah."

The priest was sitting cross-legged on the matting of our glass-enclosed veranda. He had on his black robe, with a bit of white at the neck, and looked very dusty and tired. His eyes were closed, and his lips were moving. The holy man was praying. I looked beyond him through the window to where his donkey was tied to the cherry tree. Sixteen miles on that donkey was quite a journey for an old man.

"Honorable priest," I murmured.

He opened his eyes and smiled. He remained seated, though, so I sat down next to him. "Good morning, Little Girl," he said. "The temple has been very sad without your laughter. We miss you there."

I looked at the bulky blue cloth bundle beside him. "What is it?" I asked inquisitively.

"Your honorable parent said that she would be sad not to see the persimmons ripe, and so I have brought her a branch from the tree with three beautiful ripe persimmons on it."

"Oh, she *will* be pleased," I said. "She is getting dressed and will be here any moment."

I drew closer to him. "Tell me, venerable one," I said. "How is Buddha?"

He looked rather startled. "Buddha?" he said. "Which Buddha?"

"The Buddha whose inside went away so that we could use his room, you remember?" He nodded. "Well," I continued, "how is he, did his inside come back and is everything all right? Is he himself again?"

The priest smiled gently. "Yes, Little Girl," he said, "Buddha is Buddha."

I bent forward, and lowered my voice. "Holy man," I said, "will you help me? My honorable parents may have to leave China, and they don't want to go, and I don't want to go. We all love it here. Will you help us?"

The priest looked at me inquiringly. "What can I do?"

"You are a holy man. You know Buddha, and Buddha knows you. Can't you, when you go back to the temple, ask that special Buddha who knows us to fix it so that we can stay?"

The priest shook his head. "No," he said, "I cannot ask Buddha for a foreigner."

The tears came to my eyes. "Oh, honorable, venerable, holy man!" I cried. "We are not foreigners, not really. We love Peking. We love the temple. Father speaks Mandarin. I speak Pekingese. We would like to stay forever. I know we can't stay here forever, but just ask Buddha if we can't stay a little longer." The tears were pouring down my face by now, and I bent my head to touch the floor. "Please, dear good man," I murmured, "we all love Buddha."

He touched me gently on my back. "Don't cry, Little Girl," he said, "I will think about it."

At that moment Mother came in, and the priest rose to his feet. I scuttled off to wash away my tears. I wanted no questions from Mother.

Several weeks passed. I was told nothing. I was in a fever of excitement, and I was even off my feed. Cook tried to tempt me with Mont Blanc (grated chestnuts in a mold, covered with whipped cream and glacéed chestnuts), but I could only nibble at it languidly.

Then one day when Mother and I came to fetch Father for lunch, Father looked up from the Mahan and *Jane's Fighting Ships,* which he had in front of him, and said, "I got a letter from headquarters today, Mabel."

"Come on in to lunch, we are starting with a soufflé," said Mother. So we went in and, as we were seated, Mother said, "Now, tell me."

"Well," said Father, helping himself to the spinach soufflé, "the man who was going to replace me has to stay on six months or more for another course at the War College, and so we won't be leaving just yet."

"Oh, how divine!" cried Mother. "I am so happy. Aren't you pleased, Brooke? It's a miracle, really."

I caught No. 1.'s eye as he stood behind Father's chair. "It's a miracle," I muttered in Chinese.

"What are you saying?" demanded Mother. "Speak up."

"I'm saying it's a miracle, and, Mother, may I have a special present for my birthday?"

"Your birthday!" said Mother. "Why, it won't be your birthday for ages."

"I know, but I want you to promise to take me out to the temple for a picnic on my birthday."

Mother and Father both laughed. "Of course, you silly child," said Mother. "I'd rather like to see the temple again myself. It has a very special quality about it."

"I want to ask the priest to let me have some joss sticks," I said dreamily.

Chapter 12

The Pains
of Growing Up

In spite of Buddha's interest in our affairs, it was only a reprieve, and when the early summer came we started home. We returned via Europe, although Father made a gloomy prediction that war might break out. "Brooke must see Paris and London," said Mother, and so we took the long journey home via Hong Kong, Suez, and Europe. A wonderful trip, especially Paris, as by this time I was steeped in Dumas. Henri IV and Marguerite de Valois were my twin loves.

Once in Paris, Mother started talking about Le Dix-huitième and Marie Antoinette, so I devoured every book within my comprehension on this unhappy queen. The flight to Varennes made my blood run cold, and when we went to Versailles I was so keyed up that as we stood on the balcony where Marie Antoinette had faced the Parisian mob, I could not stand it and, to my parents' disgust, insisted that I was tired and wanted to go back to the hotel. Naturally I was not indulged in this whim, and we poked into every cranny of the palace.

Mother was an ardent sightseer, and Messieurs Casenave, Pelakin, and other friends from Peking were there to show us the smartest clubs and restaurants. I saw Mother dancing the tango in a slit skirt at teatime at Armenonville and thought it very glamorous. Father and I waltzed together, but the tango seemed to be more fun, and I practiced it that evening in front of the mirror. Mother, guided by French friends, bought some lovely clothes for herself and some really jeune fille clothes for me. I was thrilled by them, as they seemed so much more sophisticated than my dresses in Peking. Little did I know what girls wore in America!

At last the trip was ended, and we were back in Washington. It was hard to settle down, but soon we installed ourselves in the little house on De Sales Street that had belonged to Father's father. It was painted a cream color and had a porch surrounded with ironwork. Best of all, on the other side of De Sales Street was a convent garden, so that we looked onto beautiful green foliage and lawn, and the entire block was lined with horse-

(previous page)
Me, dressed up with holster and hat by the Marines, at a picnic in Peking

chestnut trees. In the spring the scent of the horse-chestnut blooms drenched our little house in perfume, and in the autumn I collected horse chestnuts and polished them, then laid them in rows on the mantelpiece in my bedroom.

I had a bedroom and also a tiny sitting room, where I wrote and drew. I used to hang my poems on the walls as well as my pictures (I had begun to fancy myself as an artist as well as a writer), and it was there that eventually, when I made friends, I held the meetings of the Facio Club, of which I was founder and president. It was a literary society and, true to its name, everyone had to do something (slightly reminiscent of the Purple Cows in Peking). One of its activities was the getting out of a magazine once a month. This magazine was all hand-done. We charged five cents for a reading, and the money was given to the Band of Mercy, which was a sort of S.P.C.A.

Washington life was so different from Peking that I found it hard to adjust. In the first place, instead of a busy and complicated staff of servants, we had two colored maids, and a white maid for Mother and me. There was also a man who stoked the furnace twice a day and cleared off the sidewalk. Granny had a car and chauffeur, but we had none. And so I either had to walk or take a streetcar, or even worse, I used to go to parties, chaperoned by Catherine, the French maid, in a carriage called a Herdic. A Herdic was like a bus with seats down the sides and one climbed in from a step in the back. It had to be backed around to let you in. Even at that time it was an archaic and disappearing form of transportation, but the Herdic Company was believed by Granny and Mother to employ only ultrarespectable ex–private coachmen, and so was just the right thing for transporting a child. While other girls and boys were driving up in motorcars, I would arrive in this ancient vehicle, which took a couple of minutes to get in position in front of the house door. I would sit facing Catherine, trying to look nonchalant, but terribly aware of the curious glances and suppressed laughter.

In Washington I found the Grown-ups' life divided from the

children's life. In Peking I had been a part of my family's life, getting a cozy worm's-eye view of all that went on. But in Washington there was a complete severance. Mother had her life and I was supposed to have mine. It was only extreme diligence that kept me au courant. By sitting in the corner I was able to glean that Walt Whitman was really the poet of the people, that Nijinsky in *Le Spectre de la Rose* was like a "disembodied spirit," and that *L'Après-midi d'un Faune* was not outré, because it was so exquisitely done, and that Vorticism was the most interesting new movement afoot.

It was about this time that I went to lunch with Mr. Henry Adams. A younger relation of his had been to school with Mother, and through her, Mother met Mr. Adams. She told him that she had a daughter whom she was trying to educate and would he, a man who knew so much about education, deign to see the child. He said he would, and I went there to lunch, hardly knowing who he was or why I was there. He used to have breakfast-lunches at 12:30, when he gathered his cronies about him. I strained my ears, as I knew I was to be catechized afterward. But the conversation was mostly highly political and I was unable to understand a word. When the others had gone he took me into his little study. He was a small man, and the low sofas and chairs had been made to his measure. He was charming to me, drawing me out and talking to me as though I were Grown-up, a fact that I appreciated. As I sat facing him I noticed that the wall behind him was covered with fantastic drawings by "a man called William Blake." Mother's friend played on the clavecin and sang sixteenth- and seventeenth-century French songs for us.

Obviously this sort of thing was very poor training for mingling with boys and girls of my own age. Dancing school was a real horror for me. Once a week, Catherine and I walked up Connecticut Avenue to N Street, where the dancing class was held in a house called "the Playhouse." I walked in stout, sensible shoes, carrying my pumps in a green baize bag. Once there,

He was a small man, and the low sofas and chairs had been made to his measure. He was charming to me, drawing me out and talking to me as though I were Grown-up, a fact that I appreciated.

I changed into the pumps and advanced timidly onto the Field of Battle. Miss Hawks, the dancing mistress, was small and fat and a martinet where decorum was concerned. She stood in the middle of the floor, round as a butterball, her hair in a huge pompadour, dressed in full evening dress, her toes turned out, and with castanets in her hands. She clapped the castanets when she gave an order and called us shrilly by name. There was a musicians' gallery overhanging the room at one end, where the parents could sit and look down on us, and that made it even worse. It was bad enough to know that I was a hopeless wallflower, but to be faced with Mother's desperation on the way home was almost too much. She simply could not understand why, even in the Paul Jones, which was invented specially for wallflowers like myself, the boys avoided me.

I could not really understand it either. The boys both fascinated and bored me. We, the girls, sat on one side of the room, and they on the other. They wore knickerbockers and Norfolk jackets and long black stockings, and they looked very clean and nice, and I liked it when they held me in their rather perspiring grasp. But they had nothing to say, or at least what I had to say seemed to bore them, and they were always calling over my shoulder to someone else.

When I was confirmed in St. John's Church by Bishop Harding, Father, who was in Mexico, had written Mother to buy a suitable confirmation present for me. She had chosen to give me *Plato and Platonism* in two volumes by Walter Pater. This was a most intriguing book, and I was full of it. But it was not a book one could discuss with a boy. Boys wanted to sing a new tune, talk about Keith's Vaudeville, or hint that they had kissed many girls. It was not until I was fourteen that I really became madly interested in boys and exerted myself to please them. I found it not as difficult as I had thought. The poor creatures simply wanted to be flattered.

Of course, there was one great compensation in returning to Washington. Grandfather and Granny were there. I had seen so

The Black Spot

for April, 1916.　　Price 5ᶠ (to read)

<u>Members of the FacioLiterary Club.</u>

Brooke Russell - President

Janet Howard　　　　Frances Hopkins

Emily Watts　　　　　Adaline Pent

Janet Harlan　　　　　Priscilla Loud

little of them in the last few years that I did not remember them very well, but Grandfather had never let distance deter him. He had written constantly and sent fascinating postcards with real feather birds on them, and, at Easter, with birds popping out of satin eggs or children running into the sea. On Washington's Birthday I always got a card with a picture of General Washington, on Lincoln's Birthday a picture of Lincoln, and on the Fourth of July a card with the American flag proudly waving. He never forgot any occasion, and on my return I got a five-dollar gold piece for each of the birthdays I had missed. My English accent enchanted him especially, and Granny liked it too. I soon began to find out, though, that the Grown-ups were not quite satisfied with me. They liked me to be a child but they also wanted me to be like them. I must be a Howard, a Spence, a McGill, or even a Russell. I could not be just *me*.

Granny wanted me to be a Southern Lady, and was full of advice: "A lady never leaves her front door until her gloves are buttoned"; "A lady never crosses her legs"; "A lady never walks on the same side of the street as a gentlemen's club"; "A lady never whistles"; "A lady never speaks first to a gentleman." And so on. She was a terrible snob and I never mentioned a friend made at school that Granny wouldn't say, "Oh, that must be Sarah Worthington's granddaughter," "Oh yes, I know her, her grandmother was a White from Baltimore," or sometimes with a snort, "I never heard of them. A congressman from Ohio, oh, well!" and she would shrug her shoulders as though to say, "You can't expect *me* to know *them*."

Granny was also a money snob, and it annoyed her that her daughters, though they had married good men, had not made a great "catch." "It's that gypsy Howard look," she said, and then gazing at me, "but you have the blue eyes and golden hair of *my* family." She said it solemnly, and I knew that she expected great things of me. It was a dreadful thought, as I felt sure that I would let her down. I was such a stick-in-the-mud and unable to attract boys. This was the one bond that Granny and Mother had in common. It irritated and frightened both of them. Was I going to be like poor Aunt Marion, Father's sister, that old horror whom no one wanted around? I thought that Granny must be really whistling in the dark in trying to pin her hopes on my gray eyes and drab-colored hair, pretending that I was a blue-eyed, golden-haired Spence.

Granny was not a very realistic person; she was a reader of "light novels," a daydreamer, a weaver of fancies. We had wonderful times together. Sometimes when my family was having a party I went to Granny's right after school to spend the night in N Street. Then I really had fun. Granny and I would sit down in the Green Room, she in her upholstered velvet chair with the fringe around it, and I in the little chair Grandfather had made for me when I was four.

There was usually a coal fire burning in the grate in winter, and, as the coal smoldered, pictures would appear, and we would start our game. "What do you see in the fire, Granny?" I asked. "Well," Granny answered, "I see a lovely house, high up on a hill, with terraced gardens going down to a lake."

I looked into the fire. "Where? Show me where!"

She pointed with her tatting hook. "There." And sure enough there it was, a huge house with strange, spreading trees and dozens of terraces tumbling down the hillside. "It's my house," I announced. "And you know what, Granny?"

"What, darling?"

"Well, it's my house, and over there, see, just at the very end is your room, because you have come to live with me."

"And what's my room like?" Granny asked, knowing that we had now really got started.

"Oh, let me see. Your room is a huge room." I looked around the Green Room. "Three times as big as this, and it has six windows."

"Six windows!" Granny ejaculated.

I nodded my head solemnly. "Yes, six, because I want you to see all the gardens, and the cattle and sheep, and the beautiful lake and the fountains. And then your room, let me see . . ." I closed my eyes and tried to imagine the room. It had to be a place suitable for an older lady. Granny never used any scent except lavender water, so lavender came to my mind. "It has lavender satin walls."

"Won't satin get awfully dirty?" Granny asked practically.

I shook my head. "No, because six maids with long, covered brushes wipe it down three times a day."

"Well, that's nice," agreed Granny, tatting rapidly.

"And then it has a lavender carpet, and white taffeta curtains, and a bed like your big bed upstairs. But you know what, Granny? Instead of having plain white ruffles around the top, it's got, it's got . . ." I hesitated. I wanted something outlandishly extravagant to express what I would do for Granny. What *could* those ruffles be made of? Suddenly the idea came to me. "It's got great big white marabou ruffles," I cried, "with tassels of the purest silver."

"Goodness gracious," exclaimed Granny, "you really are spoiling me!"

"Oh, you will love it," I said, "because it has a sitting room too, where you can have tea and write your letters." I had never seen Granny write a letter, but I thought a sitting room should be used for a certain amount of writing.

"And what's my sitting room like?" she inquired.

I wanted a contrast. "It's all in black," I said.

Granny shuddered. "I don't think I like that," she said.

"But you *will* like it," I continued, quite carried away, "because the tables and chairs will all be of jade and there will be lotus buds and pomegranates in intricately wrought silver bowls. And you must leave your window open at night because the Spectre de la Rose might jump in with a great leap, or perhaps even a faun."

Granny rang the bell for Melissa. "Stuff and nonsense," she said, "I don't want a room like that. Your mother and those ridiculous friends of hers have been talking in front of you and putting absurd ideas into your head."

TWO ASTERS

—written at age ten

*T'was on an April morning,
    when
I to school did ride
I saw two lovely asters stand-
    ing side by side.
T'was on an autumn
    morning
When I to school did ride,
I saw two very withered
    stems
Standing side by side.*

*Ah t'is like a little life one
    day
So blithe and gay
Next day t'is like an autumn
    leaf
To wither, and fade away.*

This and the sketch on the opposite page are among the many drawings I did based on something I'd read about in a book or someone I'd seen on the street. These seem to be about bad weather—wind and rain.

I could not really refute it. Mother and her friend Lucretia were always talking of plates of jade and pomegranates and fauns, and I thought that I was offering Granny something very Grown-up and fine. I must have looked downcast.

"Now do you want me to tell you about when I was a little girl?" she asked.

"Oh, please," I said. This was a favorite subject. Granny had grown up in the Green Spring Valley on her father's place, which had the curious name of Stranchia. She was born in 1840 and so had had quite a long life in the pre–Civil War period. There were slaves to do everything, and life was indolent and pleasure-loving. I did not really find it interesting because it was so restricted, but at the same time it was so different that it fascinated me.

Her father always wore a gray top hat when he drove to church on Sundays, and carried two bouquets with him to hand out at the church door to two ladies who had been his friends for years. Granny's mother superintended the smoking of ham, and the making of jams and preserves, and the picking of lavender to be put in bags in the linen closet. Granny herself, at my age, went out on the street in a low, square-neck dress with short sleeves and a bonnet tied under her chin. The idea of short sleeves on the street interested me tremendously. I thought only high necks and long sleeves permissible, never having seen anything else. Until after the Civil War Granny had never picked up anything from the floor. If she was sitting on a chair and dropped a handkerchief, she rang a bell for a slave to come and retrieve it.

I had read *Uncle Tom's Cabin* and the idea of slaves did not appeal to me. "I'm glad there aren't slaves anymore," I said, "I think it was an awful thing."

"You are talking like a damnyankee," said Granny crossly. "You don't know anything about it. They were all so happy at Stranchia, singing all day on the plantation and dancing and singing in their cabins at night. Look at Aunt Nancy, don't you think she is happy?"

Aunt Nancy, who was now Granny's cook and the only one to remain with them, had been the Topsy to Granny's Eva. I had to admit that Aunt Nancy was happy. In fact, at times, she seemed a little too happy, when she drank mysteriously from a stone jug and smoked her pipe and danced a jig. She was a bit of a shrew. But my mind was not changed about slavery. I hated the whole thing. Two horrible boys I had known in Newport had a record, which they played endlessly on their gramophone, of Uncle Tom pleading with Simon Legree. That and the book had convinced me once and for all that I was an abolitionist. Granny still spoke bitterly about the North and the War between the States. She looked upon all Yankees with disfavor and was glad that Father had some Southern blood in him.

Granny made history seem very near, and although her viewpoint was narrow and her recollections rather frivolous, they had a great impact on me.

When we heard Grandfather's key in the door we immediately stopped our game. "Are you there, Bertie?" he would call as he came through the velvet portieres.

"Yes, Mr. Howard," Granny answered, "right here in the Green Room with Brooke."

"Why, in heaven's name, won't you call me George?" demanded Grandfather irascibly.

"Law, Mr. Howard," said Granny, "this is the way I was brought up as a young lady."

"You are not a young lady anymore," growled Grandfather. "After forty years of marriage and six children, I should think that you could use my Christian name."

Granny laughed and said nothing. Grandfather kissed me and made me giggle because of his tickling beard. "Would you like me to read *The Pit and the Pendulum* or some Sherlock Holmes, Brooke?" he asked.

"Oh, let's have *The Hound of the Baskervilles,*" I said. "Remember, you have just started it?"

"All right, come up to the Morning Room," he said and started upstairs.

The Morning Room, so called because it got the morning sun, had an upright rosewood piano and some bookcases, and some stiff sofas, and two round, fat, deliciously comfortable chairs. Grandfather sat in one and I in the other. And off we went into a world of horror and fear. Grandfather was a lawyer, and in his off moments was busy writing a study of Crime and Criminals, so he liked to keep his hand in by reading Conan Doyle and Poe and Wilkie Collins. Sometimes he read me bits of what he was writing and I grew to know well the Edinburgh students who dug up corpses, and the man who killed his wives in bathtubs, and the one who chopped his wife up and threw her out of a porthole, and a whole group of fiendish and usually unapprehended characters.

Grandfather's other interests were Shakespeare and English madrigals, carpentry and the Metropolitan Club. Every Sunday after attending service at St. Matthew's Catholic Church, he stopped at the Metropolitan Club. My parents and I often had lunch with my grandparents at two o'clock on Sundays, and many times Grandfather was late because he had lingered over a sherry with a crony at the club. "Drat that old club!" Granny would exclaim, worrying about the food getting cold. But when Grandfather came he often had interesting things to tell us. "I had a long talk with So-and-so," he would say. "He is a vain man, a limited man, a damned fool, but I like him." The luncheons were colossal, as Granny had the Southern idea of a groaning board. Sometimes it would be after four o'clock before we got up from the table, and even I would be sleepy.

On the banner nights I spent with them my grandparents let me stay up later than I did at home and I had the fun of watching Melissa put a brass warming pan with a long handle on it into their bed to warm up the sheets. Grandfather had a little stand to hang his big gold watch on, as he considered it bad for a watch to lay it down flat. He wore a nightcap and a nightshirt, and Granny wore long-sleeved nightgowns, with a ruffle around the wrists and around her neck. They climbed up two little velvet-covered steps to get into their bed, and although they had a bathroom right next door, they had a wooden box called a "commode" close by their bed.

At breakfast they had kidney stew and waffles, or chops and hot rolls and fried potatoes. I loved it all and drank in every detail of their habits.

When the weather grew warm Granny wore a muslin wrapper around the house and fanned herself continuously with a painted fan on a long stick. She gave up her heavy diet and ate practically nothing but sliced tomatoes and ice-cold watermelon. She hated the heat and usually went off as soon as she could to their place, Greystone, in the Blue Ridge Mountains.

As I have said, Granny's desire was to have me a Southern Lady, "The Belle of My Year," and to make a good marriage. On the other hand, Grandfather was not concerned about my future. He and I had our communion in crime. Mother, of course, was the most concerned of all, but I learned that Father, too, had a fixation about me, and for me. He could not bear to see me reading or writing poetry. His sister May long ago had met a man at a summer place called Cazenovia, New York, where Father's parents had a house. She was a sweet young thing, with long brown hair and a gentle smile. The man turned out to be a frightful cad, for he won her heart and then threw her over. Poor Aunt May could not recover from this experience. She took to reading poetry night and day and finally pined away and died. This made an indelible impression on Father, and when he saw me curled up with Walt Whitman or Swinburne or Byron or, worse still, writing poetry myself, he would seek Mother out. "Something ought to be done about Brooke," he would say. "It isn't healthy to want to stay indoors with her nose in a book, particularly a poetry book. She ought to be out on a bicycle."

He tried to teach me to ride a bicycle, but I seemed to have no sense of balance and fell off almost as soon as I got on. He tried to teach me to play tennis, being a beautiful player himself, but I was impossible. I used to stand stupidly in the middle of the court watching the ball so intently that I forgot I was supposed to hit back. Though Father loved me dearly, I must have disappointed him in many ways as a child. In order to combat my love of poetry, and perhaps to recapture his own boyhood, he gave me books that *he* liked. So I ended up with a whole shelf of *Masterman Ready, Midshipman Easy, Two Years Before the Mast, Around the World in Eighty Days* (in fact *all* of Jules Verne), *Tom Brown's School Days, The Wreck of the Grosvenor, Barlasch of the Guard,* and a book of *Poems for Patriots.* These were the books I should read, Father thought, although of course to him anything that Mother liked *must* be right. He considered her taste in everything impeccable.

As for Mother, she wanted me to be many things. She wanted me intelligent, pretty, graceful, well-mannered, responsive, quiet, gay, good-humored, and when with children of my own age, the life of the party. I was not stupid, and my sycophantic desire to please made me a good student (in everything, that is, but mathematics; when Father was ordered away and could not help me with my homework, I had to give up mathematics entirely). I *did* have nice manners, I was always hopping around waiting on the Grown-ups, smiling brightly and making my curtsy. This curtsy was so ingrained in me that when I married at sixteen, and was on my own, I still was bobbing up and down to old women of twenty and twenty-five. But I failed utterly in being pretty or graceful, or the life of the party. Even with girls my own age I could hold my own only if I knew them well. As I grew older I affected the habit of wearing some distinctive bit of adornment—a special sort of belt, or something around my neck like amber and coral beads mixed; at one time I would never wear anything but a Glengarry cap perched on the side of my head. I rather liked making a clown of myself,

Though Father loved me dearly, I must have disappointed him in many ways as a child. In order to combat my love of poetry, and perhaps to recapture his own boyhood, he gave me books that he *liked....*

and when with my own "set" would do almost anything for a laugh.

When we first arrived in Washington, however, I was still as shy with children my own age as I had been at Newport, and my greatest comfort was my dolls, who had come all the way from China with me. They were a substitute for the brothers and sisters I had never had, and the friends I had never had time to make. There were five of them: Geraldine, a life-sized doll, Evie, a huge wax doll with real hair, Harry, a baby doll, Rachel, the Manchu doll, and Priscilla, a rag doll—the best loved— whose face had been kissed away, leaving only one bright blue eye which had to be fastened on with a pin. I loved them all, and when I was at home a great part of my time was taken up in dressing them, feeding them, putting them to bed, and talking to them. Actually, putting them to bed was a farce, because after the Grown-ups were out of the way, they all wound up in my bed.

One particular day we were having tea and they were all sitting on the sofa in front of me. I was reading them a poem I had just written:

THE WAVES
Oh what are the waves a-saying
When they rise dark and high?
Oh what are the waves a-saying
As they pass slowly by?
Oh tis they that have a secret
Way down in the mystic deep
A very wonderful secret
Which no one else could keep.

Geraldine had slipped down onto the pillow and her eyes were closed. She looked dreadfully bored. I shook her rather crossly and her eyes opened. "Sit up," I said, "and listen to my poem. You are being very rude."

"Brooke," Mother's voice floated up to me from her sitting room, which was just under my bedroom.

"Yes, Mother," I answered.

"What are you doing up there?" she asked.

"Nothing."

"But you must be doing something, I heard you talking."

"I wasn't doing anything."

"Well, if you aren't doing anything, come down and I will read some *Ivanhoe* to you."

I sighed deeply and whispered good-bye to the dolls. Priscilla's blue eye looked at me consolingly. "Don't worry," she seemed to say, "we will be here when you come back."

Mother was sitting in the cushion-filled wicker chair in the bay window and had the red leather copy of *Ivanhoe* in her hand. She looked up laughing when I came in.

"Were you playing with those ridiculous dolls again?" she asked.

"No, I was reading them a poem I had written," I said aggressively.

"Now, don't get beyond yourself," said Mother sharply. "You know perfectly well that reading to them is playing with them, and you are really much too big to play with dolls. You are eleven years old and you look silly playing with dolls like a baby."

"Nobody sees me," I muttered sullenly.

"I see you," Mother replied, "and I don't like it a bit. At your age I was out skipping rope and playing games, and having all sorts of fun. I don't see why you have to be such a stick-in-the-mud, moping about the house, talking to those dolls. I wish that we had never brought them back from China."

"Why, we couldn't *leave* them!" I cried out in horror.

"Oh, yes, we could have, just the way we left the dogs, and that's exactly what we should have done, but let's forget about that now. Sit down and I'll start reading. Do you remember where we left off?"

"Ivanhoe had just entered the lists at Ashby-de-la-Zouche," I repeated dully. It took me several minutes to bring my attention to the story. The callousness of Mother's remarks appalled me.

Leave my darling dolls in China, what a terrible thought! Leaving the dogs had been a bitter blow; but it had been explained to me that we were coming home via England, and no dogs were allowed in England.

(opposite)
"Seen on the Stage"
(from my sketch book)

Everything went smoothly for the next few days, and no mention was made of my silly habits, even though I had been caught by Catherine serving tea to the dolls.

Then one day that week I came home late from school. I had had lunch with my grandmother and Catherine came to fetch me there. As we walked home I sensed a sort of smugness in her. She kept smiling to herself, and finally threw out a hint that things would be different at home. *Something* had happened that day.

"Dîtes-moi, what is it?" I demanded. But she refused to tell me. I hurried along faster, faster, knowing that she could not keep up with me in her tight skirt. At each street crossing she had to scream at me to wait for her. I pretended that I was going to dash across by myself, but fear always brought me back to the curb. I did not want to tempt Providence too far. We arrived home in a very bad humor and I stalked up the stairs to my room, leaving Catherine behind me. I went directly to the closet and hung up my coat and hat, then turned back to the room. . . .

"Really, Priscilla," I said, "Catherine is impossible. She is getting beyond herself." I looked at the sofa as I said it and suddenly realized that the sofa was empty. Dismayed and terrified, I frantically searched the room, under the sofa, under the bed, behind the bureau, and the bookcase. Not a sign of one of them. As I got up from my knees I saw Catherine standing in the doorway, laughing.

"Gone," she said, "Parti."

"What do you mean, gone?" I demanded. "Where could they go?"

"Your mother gave them away," she said. "The Salvation Army came for many things and they also took the dolls."

I could not even cry. I simply looked at her. At the moment her squat figure and swarthy face seemed the devil incarnate to me.

Types de femmes mondaines
modernes.
Mal-saines — moralement
physiqu...

Only $5 a week!!!
and no beaux!
(From "Pollow Ditz")

— Seen on the Stage —

it wasn't
to her beaux
a "?.
for —
Pollies)

"I don't believe it," I said, a cold chill gripping my heart. "I don't believe it. You are just a horrid mean old woman."

Catherine shrugged and turned away. "Madame will be home soon," she said, "and she will tell you."

I threw myself on my bed and buried my face deep in the pillow. To lose the dogs, to lose Ginger, my horse, and Amah and Mafoo, and now my dearly loved, faithful dolls!

It was more than I could bear. I began to cry, and could not stop. I do not know how long I cried, but it was dark when I felt Mother's arms around me.

"Don't, darling. Don't, Brooke," she was saying. "I only did it for your own good."

"Leave me alone," I wailed, kicking my feet up and down on the bed. "Go away. I hate you."

"No, no, no," said Mother. "Don't be a baby, Brooke. You must start growing up."

"I don't *want* to grow up," I sobbed. "I want to stay a child. Oh, do leave me alone. Who will ever love Priscilla? They may throw her away because she hasn't any face."

"Oh, no," said Mother consolingly. "They won't do that. Some poor little girl whose family can't buy her a doll will get Priscilla, and you, darling, must start making friends, and have friends to play with instead of dolls."

I understood the hypocrisy of Grown-ups and knew that Mother did not believe that a new little girl would love Priscilla any more than I believed it. I buried my face deeper in the pillow, and shaking Mother's hand off, gave way to choking sobs. After a while Mother grew discouraged and went away. Then I sat up to look at the empty sofa. A ray from the streetlight illuminated it, and made its emptiness colder than ever. I went over and knelt down. "Dear God," I prayed, "please let them be happy, and let them know I will love them always. Amen."

Peking Diary

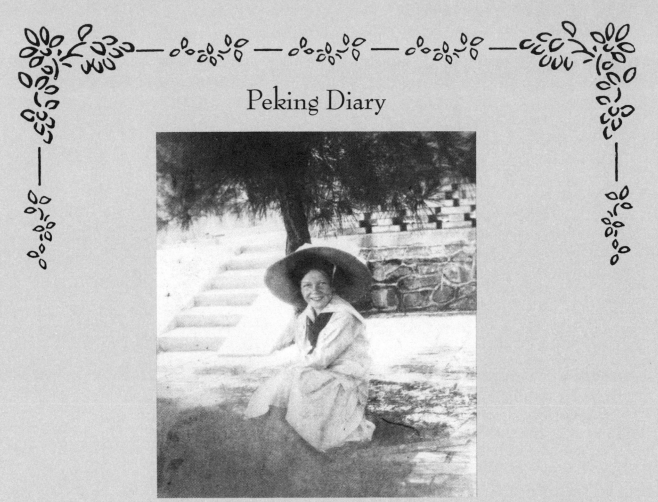

In Peking at the Temple of One Hundred Courtyards

Author's note: This diary was written aboard the *Tango Maru*, a Japanese ship that took us from China to France. Away from the influence of Peking, my viewpoint began to change. I was no longer a pet of the legation; I was on my own and felt I had to prove myself and please other people.

My birthday. Went to say good-bye to the Hills. Went to Chen Ching Chi, and Chang Ong Su, two temples in the Western Hills.

The time draws near for the return to America and the last days are very sad ... In the morning I saw Darlingo [The bugler Johnny Malone]. In the afternoon we had a paper doll wedding. The cook made a cake.

Went for a long walk with the dogs. Gyp was so cute, he played with the little red dog. O, I hate to leave him. I wrote to the President asking if I could bring him to America, but Father says it is England that would not let him in.

There is hardly anything left in our house, everything is packed. Alas—the world is a dreary place.

Had my last music lesson. Saw my Darlingo. Spoke to him. Said "Hello." Oh, I don't want to leave Peking, my pony, Gyp, Darlingo, Amah, the coolies, Boys, and Cooks. Went to the Temple of the Moon.

Cried to-day. Sat on Mother's lap. She told me a story.... Came home, and found a lot of people for tea to-day to say good-bye.

Parted with Gyp, the darling of my heart. Oh I love him so. O Gyp, Gyp POORBA. Oh I am so sad.

Started away. All the legation people down to see us off. The band played. O Gyp, where are you? O so dreadfully sorry to go.

O Yangtze River, a little seasick.

Set sail—rather—left Shanghai, awfully sorry to leave. The Tango Maru is a nice ship. There are two Swiss on board and a rather nice Urasian [sic] woman who plays the piano beautifully. She's awfully pretty.

Reached Hong Kong. It is quite nice. Awfully quaint with little slanting streets. Went up to the peak in full funicular. It's lovely up there. Mother was scared. We came down in sedan chairs.

Stayed in Hong Kong. 4 new children on board. Had lessons, quite hard, only two sums.

At sea The most beautiful sunset today, green on the right, gray above with the red sun peeping out in the middle, gold orange, pink blue lavender all over.

Reached Singapore. Went to the American consul, Mr. C., and Mrs. C. gave me a doll. Drove through the country.

Still at Singapore. Mother and Father went ashore, but I didn't. A great many peddlers came on board, and I bought a piece of coral.

Reached Penang, Malay Straits. It is a very dirty place. Went to the Chinese Temple. It is not very nice, but the Botanical Gardens are. All the roads are red and there are lots of rubber trees.

Left dirty Penang. Seas rough.

Reached Colombo, Ceylon. It is a very pretty place. It has no real harbor, only a made one. We went for a drive, then to Mrs. Simpson's for tea. She has two dogs.

Went ashore 9:30. Went shopping bought a lovely elephant. Went to Mrs. Simpson's to tiffin. Had Ceylon curry. All the boys wear turbins [sic].

At sea Many passengers are seasick.

Very rough. They call the wind a monsoon. Passed Socotra, but many miles off so that we could not see it. Mr. Madden is still seasick. Oh it's funny.

June 12 Reached Gulf of Aden. Nice and quite calm. Had a lovely swimming bath, but it is getting rather hot. Mother's wedding anniversary.

Not so hot after all, quite cool in fact in the Gulf of Aden.

Passed Perim Island and entered into the Red Sea.

June 19 Reached Suez and stayed 3 hours. The Suez Canal is very interesting, but there are many flies, and my eyes hurt. We saw many camels.

June 20 Reached Port Said, did not go ashore. Father and Mother did, and did not come back until 3 minutes to 9. They had to come in a special boat and I cried I was so frightened.

June 23 We passed through the Straits of Messina. We saw ruins from the earthquake. Also orange groves. Saw two towns Regno [Reggio] and Villgeorana [Villa San Giovanni] which are very pretty places and Messina which is on Sicily and is not pretty. Saw Etna smoking. Passed Stromboli, and saw it smoking too.

Supposed to reach Marseilles, but we are one day late. Had a lovely Captain's dinner.

Passed between Corsica and Sardinia, not very pretty.

Passed the Château d'Iff. Landed in Marseilles.

Left for Paris. Reached Lyon a silk center. It is a big place with a beautiful church. Burgundy is a beautiful country. Reached Paris at 10 p.m. Went to Hôtel Normandie.

Went to the Grand Magasin du Louvre and bought a very pretty hat and dress. Met Mr. C. who took us for a drive.

To-day there is a taxicab strike. Went for a walk in the Jardin des Tuileries, which is very pretty. Had my hair done a new way. Went to Notre Dame in the morning. It is a beautiful cathedral, with figures of all the saints on it, and funny looking things on the top. Also saw the Bastille. In the afternoon went to Versailles, Petite Trianon, and Grande Trianon. Saw all of Marie Antoinette's rooms. O, how sad.

In the morning went to the Tombe de Napoleon, in the afternoon went to the Louvre. Saw the most beautiful pictures ever seen. I think Rubens' are the nicest.

We went to the Hôtel de Cluny, and saw shoes, dresses, hats, books, of all ages. It is a beautiful place. It is cold to-day. Mother has bought some lovely dresses, and a yellow suit with a waistcoat.

Went to the Luxembourg. Saw pictures that were not very pretty, but were very new. Father and Mother went to the Russian balley. I think the French are very horrid.*

---

*The young author had an unfortunate experience while her family were out, and the visiting maid down at her supper. The little girl undressed, walked around the room in her bare skin, and used the pôt de chambre. While on this receptacle, she looked out the window (she had forgotten to draw the shade), and there across the courtyard at another window, stood a man with a pair of binoculars trained on her. Her reaction was instantaneous. She stuck out her tongue, and raised her small hand to her nose in a gesture of derision, and kept it there until the Peeping Tom, losing his nerve, lowered his glasses, and pulled down his shade. This episode poisoned Paris for her, and her family had a hard time inducing her to go out on the streets. She was afraid of coming face to face with him, and cried a great deal.

Went to the Bon Marché had tea with Lady ffrench. She gave Mother her picture. We leave to-morrow.

Left for London, crossed the Channel, and was not a bit seasick. Father says it's because Neptune baptized me on the Tango Maru. It was raining when we reached London. Had my first tea in London. It seems vast to me, and I feel small in it.

Went to Westminster Abbey to a service, it is a beautiful place very tall and magnificent with the graves with the statues over them all around. Went to Hampton Court. Walked in the maze which is exciting. Had tea at a little inn called "The King's Arms."

Went to Father's tailor, and got him an out-fit. Afterwards went to Cooks. In the afternoon went to St. Paul's Church, and heard the little boys sing. Also went to the Tower of London. So sorry for the little Princes.

In the morning went to the National Gallery, and saw the most perfect picture in the world by Raphael. Went for a walk to the Burlington Arcade. Had my purse stolen there. Went for a bus ride to the very heart of London. Cried about my purse. It was new in Paris.

In the morning went to the British Museum, and saw bits of the Temple of Diana, the most important part of which was the Pantheon, and the other was the Acropolis.

Went to the Victoria and Albert Museum. Saw beautiful old wood carvings of many sorts, old fireplaces, statues of every description. I like the English.

In the morning went shopping until 15 to 12. Then we went to the station. Got on a train and went to the Tillbury Docks, got on the boat and pulled off.

Distance was 231. Light S.W. wind. Smooth sea—nothing in particular happened.

July 21 Reached New York. Went for a drive up 5th Ave. It's not as nice as London. I got 4 new dresses. At 3:30 we left New York for Washington. Grandfather met us at the train. Grandmother came up from the country, it's awfully hot. I don't understand about American sums.

September 13 Moved into our new house. It's darling. I have the cutest little room with such funny little windows.

October 1 Began school. I'm in the 6th and 7th grades. I like it quite well, not very, not as nice as Peking, of course I have not really met the other children yet.

Some of the girls laughed at me to-day. They say I speak queerly. I didn't cry.

Wonderful surprise. When I came home from school there was Nicky, a dear little bull-dog. Father and Mother gave him to me. O, I am so happy.

Chapter 13

Grown-ups
Are Best in the
Drawing Room

When I was thirteen I started to change. I began to have more real friends. In fact, I became a member, perhaps even a leader, of a set. I was the most literary of that particular group, as the passion for reading, once aroused, can be consuming, and as I read I also wrote, filling page after page of yellow foolscap with novels, plays, and poems. I wanted to be a writer above all things, but I also wanted to remain "one of the pack," and I did.

We had our Secrets, our Literary Society, our books in which we wrote our favorite girl's name, boy's name, flower, author, etc. We dressed as nearly alike as possible, and we were given to laughing uncontrollably when together. We spoke a language called "Tuten" and used certain words to express our likes and dislikes. We met at each other's houses almost every afternoon, and usually paid our "party calls" together. The party call was to our minds a wonderful invention, but to me now it seems more like an invention of the devil himself. After a person gave a party, the next Saturday she had to stay at home to receive visits from guests who had been at the party, and who turned out en masse to thank their host or hostess. Tea or lemonade and cakes were served, and someone usually played the piano while the rest stood around and sang. It sounds ghastly to think of having two consecutive parties, but that was the thing and we all looked forward to the party call.

I still hung over the banisters and listened to Mother in the drawing room, but not quite as much. Mother's friend Monsieur Casenave had come to America on a mission headed up by André Tardieu and Edouard de Billy. Father was away and Mother was alone and bored, so they and many other friends came almost every afternoon at tea or cocktail time. Occasionally my name was mentioned, and then I would prick up my ears and lean over as far as I could in order to hear.

"But chère amie," I heard Monsieur Casenave say, "you must discuss things more with Brooke. You must not allow her to have a keyhole philosophy of life."

"Oh, she reads everything," said Mother. "I am sure that she knows more than she appears to but I want her to be innocent. It is very appealing."

"Ah, yes," agreed Monsieur Casenave, "but not innocent forever. That which is innocence in a growing girl is ignorance in a woman of thirty." They all laughed heartily at that and I went back to my room. What boring talk! I recorded it in my diary because I had the soul of a Pepys, but I much preferred Mother on a loftier note or else the conversation of my own friends. I had become rather censorious of Mother. I did not like her Peking habit of smoking and pointedly looked away when she lit a cigarette. "Madame Bakmetchef, the wife of the Russian ambassador, always smokes in public," said Mother. But I still disapproved. I did not like her frivolous hats and wanted her to wear a prim toque with a heavy veil fastened neatly at her neck and her hair combed severely back instead of curling all over her head. I looked with a jaundiced eye on the books and flowers and notes that were constantly arriving at the house. In fact, I wanted Mother to be a cozy frump. I could not explain why; I knew that a lady could accept books and flowers from a gentleman and that, even though Father was away, Granny and Grandfather were just around the corner, and that whatever Mother did would be quite all right. In fact, I could not even imagine why I felt the way I did. But my hackles rose in proportion to the sounds of merriment from the drawing room. My sour face irritated Mother and she would stamp her foot and say, "Why are you so sullen? *Why* do you dislike all my friends? It is terrible for me to have such a sulky, bad-tempered child. Heaven knows I have done everything in the world for you."

Part of my grievance was that, as I wanted Mother to look and act like a New England schoolmistress, Mother in her turn wanted me to be a completely un-American foreign child. I wore high-laced shoes to keep my ankles small when other girls were wearing oxfords. I wore bronze pumps at dancing class and a bronze bow in my hair when everyone else wore patent-leather slippers and *no* bow. But worse than that, while I was wearing

When I was thirteen I started to change. I began to have more real friends. . . . I became a member, perhaps even a leader, of a set. I was the most literary of that particular group, as the passion for reading, once aroused, can be consuming, and as I read I also wrote, filling page after page of yellow foolscap with novels, plays, and poems. I wanted to be a writer above all things, but I also wanted to remain "one of the pack . . ."

We had our Secrets, our Literary Society, our books in which we wrote our favorite girl's name, boy's name, flower, author, etc.

to parties perfectly straight velvet dresses with lace collars and cuffs, the other girls were beginning to wear low-necked dresses and carry ostrich feather fans. I looked the dowdy jeune fille and could imagine that I was rapidly becoming like Father's sister Marion. This was a depressing thought. I was still not popular with boys (much to Mother's disgust) because I was overcome with shyness and had no "line." But I sensed that if I were dressed a little bit more snappily I would have a better chance. Boys did not set much store by a real lace collar and an infinitesimal string of real pearls. Boys wanted something more spectacular. Some of the girls I knew had even been kissed by boys, and although Mother and Grandmother told me that boys did not really like girls "*like that,*" I thought that they—Mother and Grandmother—were perhaps not quite up-to-date in their thinking. In any event I was determined not to continue in the shapeless velvets. There was to be a dance at the house of a friend before we all went away for the summer and I made up my mind that, come hell or high water, I would have a more Grown-up dress to wear or I just would not go.

I approached Grandmother first. I usually lunched with her once a week after school, and that day I lingered on after lunch, sitting with her by the fire in the Green Room. I sighed deeply as I looked into the fire, a long, deep, quivering sigh. Granny looked up from her needlework. "What is the matter, Brooke?" she said. "Have you indigestion?"

"No, Granny dear," I answered, and sighed again deeply.

"For goodness' sake, child, what *is* the matter?" said Granny, pulling her needle sharply in and out of the canvas. "Tell Granny."

I shook my head mournfully. "It's no use," I said.

"No use, what is no use? What do you mean?"

"It's no use telling you. It won't do any good." And I looked sadly into the fire. Granny laid down her needle. "Brooke," she said, "why can't you tell me? There is nothing you can't tell your own granny."

I had heard this before from Grown-ups and I knew from experience that it was the sign of the greatest curiosity and, if cautious, you could do almost anything with them until their curiosity was satisfied. "No, Granny," I said, "it really isn't any use. Besides, Mother would be very cross."

Granny pricked up her ears at that. She had, I gathered, been a veritable tatar with her own children, but now she was often furious with Mother for being too severe with me. "Dearest," she said, "you just tell your old granny, and it will be a secret between us. We won't tell Mother a thing about it. What is it, darling?" She laid down her needle again and, beaming, laid a hand on my head. "Dear, dear child," she said, "tell your old granny."

I looked up into her bright blue eyes and let my lips quiver a bit. "Oh, Granny," I said, "I'm awfully unhappy."

This was too much. She threw her arms around my neck, and I crept close to her. "Precious," she murmured, "precious, precious Brooke." I let her rock me back and forth, and I hugged her hard in return. Granny really was a sweetie and I loved our chats by the fire.

Finally, she let me go and I sat back on the footstool. "I will tell you, Granny darling," I said. "I want an evening dress to wear at Louise's dance."

"An evening dress?" Granny took off her glasses. "What do you mean by an evening dress? You're only thirteen."

"Thirteen and a half," I prompted. "And what I want is something with short sleeves and a heart-shaped neckline. I just can't go to parties anymore, Granny, with a dress up to my neck and long sleeves. I look ridiculous and no one will dance with me."

"Boys don't really like—" began Granny.

"Please, Granny, don't say that," I said. "I don't want to go around all over the place kissing boys but I'd like to have them dance with me."

"Goodness," said Granny. "Are you *still* a wallflower?" She had not been to dancing class lately and so perhaps had hopes that things had changed.

"Yes, I am," I said. "I guess it's partly because I am a bad dancer and have no line. But it's also because I wear such queer clothes."

"What's a line?" said Granny, taking a sip of Vichy water.

"Oh, it's being able to talk about funny things. Being smart and flip and knowing all sorts of jokes, saying things you don't mean."

"Can't you do that?" demanded Granny sharply.

"No, I can't," I said sadly. "I just can't. When a boy dances with me I can smell him. I know if he uses Ivory soap or Cuticura. But I just haven't a thing to say to him."

"Well, I declare!" observed Granny. "That's terrible. All Howards can talk. What's the matter with you?"

"I don't know," I said. "I try terribly hard, but the more I try the worse it gets. I tell you, Granny, I can smell them but I can't talk to them."

"Do you think an evening dress would help?" she demanded.

"Oh, I do!" I answered. "I would *look* more like other girls and so I could *be* more like them."

Granny sewed for a few minutes without speaking. And I looked gloomily into the fire. Finally she spoke: "I'll speak to your mother. And if she says yes, I will give you the prettiest evening dress we can buy or Stella can make."

I leapt from the footstool with joy and flung my arms around her neck. "Darling, darling Granny," I cried, "thank you, thank you, thank you!"

That night Granny called Mother on the telephone and, although I was supposed to be doing my homework, my ears were flattened back straining to hear the conversation. Mother's ejaculations of "Really!" "How absurd!" "Ridiculous!" didn't reassure me. And when she finally hung up and turned to me, I knew I was in for it.

"Brooke," she said, "what is all this absurd talk you've been having with your grandmother?"

Seen in a Ballroom:
"The Old Beau"

"What do you mean, Mother?" I said, bending studiously over my homework.

"Look at me," said Mother. I lifted my head and looked at her. "Now," she said, "just what is it you were telling your grandmother?"

"Nothing much," I mumbled, scribbling on the page in front of me. "Oh, yes, you were," said Mother. "You were saying that you weren't properly dressed, and that you looked absurd, and that no boys would dance with you. Isn't that what you said? Answer me."

I looked up. "Yes, that's what I said. Granny is right. I just hate those velvet dresses. That's what I told her."

Mother lit a cigarette and I looked away. "If you only knew," she said, "the compliments I get about the way you are dressed. Lady Spring-Rice and Madame Jusserand, and all the people who really know, think that you look just right, so different from—"

I interrupted. "That's just it, Mother!" I cried. "I look different. I don't want to be different. I want to be like everybody else."

Mother put out the newly lighted cigarette in an ashtray. "You are hopeless," she said. "But I suppose if you insist on being like everyone else you might as well be. I have certainly tried to do my best. We will go down to Garfinckel's tomorrow. Your grandmother, whom you seem to be able to twist around your finger, says that she will give you a dress as a present. She is ruining you. *I* give up." And she walked out of the room.

A few days later we went to Garfinckel's and almost at once I saw just the dress I wanted. It was pale-pink taffeta with puff sleeves, a square neck, and a bunch of blue velvet cherries at the waist. I was ecstatic about it. And when the night of the party came and I put it on, the whole household gaped at me admiringly. I still had the bronze slippers and the bronze hair ribbon, but I forgot them in the excitement of short sleeves and square neckline. It was a little loose around the neck, but I did not care, as it fitted tightly about my waist and was not a shapeless velvet

Seen in a Ballroom: The girl he was asked to be nice to (note the tapping foot)

sack. Alas, one swallow does not make a summer. And one new dress did not turn me into the belle of the ball. There was, however, one boy who danced with me several times and asked me to have the supper dance with him. So, when supper came around, we went to the buffet and after filling our plates, we went to sit on the stairs. He sat on the stairs above me and kept leaning over to whisper in my ear. I thought him quite funny and began to discover that I could be funny, too. So we talked back and forth until, turning my head suddenly to look at him, I found that instead of looking at my face, he was staring down the gaping neckline of my dress. I followed his glance and looked in horror at my bosom, which in the last six months had grown out of proportion to the rest of me. I never thought that it would be of interest to anybody, but his inquisitive look made it suddenly a thing of horror and shame to me. I hated my bosom, my dress, and him. I put down my plate and pressed my hands against the neckline of my dress.

"Oh, don't be a spoilsport," he said, laughing. "I wasn't doing anything," and he hummed, "I'm Always Chasing Rainbows."

"I think you are a horrid boy," I said furiously. "I don't like you at all." I got up, and moving through the crowd found my way to the coatroom. It was so early that Catherine had not yet come to fetch me, and I waited there blinking back my tears until her arrival.

We returned home in silence. Mother was at the door and opened it at the sound of our footsteps. "Darling," she cried gaily, "did you have a good time?"

I flung myself into her arms. "No," I said weeping. "And you were right, Mother. Those velvet dresses are much better. I never want to wear this dress again. I don't want to be Grown-up!"

Mother was almost too surprised to comment. "For heaven's sake," she said finally, giving me a pat. "You really are a queer child. Now run along to bed."

After this bit of leniency and wisdom on Mother's part, I did not continue to try to change her into a New England

schoolmistress and was content to be dressed in whatever pleased her. I realized that she was wiser than I. I was still not ready to grow up and I went back to smiling at her friends and acting out "La Cigale et La Fourmi" for them at teatime. It made things easier to be in one's proper place in life.

It was the summer after my "new look" that I went away from home on my first visit by myself and had another disturbing experience. There was a girl I knew in Washington who did not go to school with me, as she was being brought up by a governess. Her aunt, with whom she lived (her mother was dead), was a friend of Mother's and, contrary to my usual habit of disliking all friends picked out for me by Mother, I grew very fond of her. She was not a friend of any of the other girls I knew, she was not a member of the Facio Club, and she never read a book or wrote a story, but she used to laugh at everything I said, which naturally endeared her to me. Her aunt liked the way I dressed so much that she had the same dress made for Anna and it was fun to walk along Connecticut Avenue together, dressed as twins. It sent us into gales of laughter to see people looking at

In the drawing room: The young man is being difficult.

us, and we invented different ways of laughing, which we then practiced over the telephone. She really brought out the very silliest side of me but she never seemed to irritate Mother. I suppose it was because her aunt was extremely well bred and chic, and they lived in a most enchanting house on Massachusetts Avenue. It was the first house that I really ever noticed, aside from our own, and I loved it. It had a room on the ground floor, which opened onto a garden, the walls of which were covered with a beautiful Chinese wallpaper. I thought it the prettiest room I had ever seen because it was so gay and the soft colors of the wallpaper were repeated in the bowls of fresh flowers that were everywhere. On the second floor there was a ballroom, all white and gold, with pale-green taffeta curtains and white and gold banquettes around the walls. I drank it all in, every detail of the elegance fascinated me. It was like the houses I used to see in the fire in Granny's house. It smelled delicious, too, of wax and potpourri, and I always liked nice smells.

In the summer Anna went with her aunt to the family house on Long Island, and this summer she asked if I could come for a couple of weeks. Mother was delighted, and accepted at once. She admired Miss L. enormously and Anna, she said, was brought up the way she would like to have brought me up. (Mother thought it much more chic to have a governess at home than to go to Miss Madeira's School.) I don't think she realized that Miss Stringfellow, Anna's governess, was almost as uneducated as Anna, and that the main ambition of governess and pupil was to go to the races at Pimlico with a friend of Anna's father. Miss Stringfellow was mad for racing and consulted the Ouija board, which often told her which horse to back. Mother liked Anna's pretty voice and nice manners and attractive background and, as I say, I liked her because she used to roar with laughter at my sallies and implore me to "just say it once more." I considered myself quite a wit, and though I knew I was not as funny as all that, still it is reassuring to deceive oneself a bit.

*A good dancer,
but the wrong size.*

Anna's aunt was one of the people I admired most. She was not beautiful like Mother's friend Miss Clara E. or intellectual like her friend Lucretia, but she was extremely elegant, always turned out perfectly, every hair in place, and her jewelry sparkling. I loved the blue satin covers in all her bureau drawers and the sable lap robe in her electric brougham, and her hats standing in her closet on their blue satin hat stands. In spite of all this luxury, she was rather an austere person. I knew even then that she had these things because they were what she *should* have, and not because she prized them. She was very precise and very strict, but she was also extremely kind, and I loved picking up her handkerchief or running to do some small errand for her.

The decision to accept the invitation was a momentous one. I was not quite sure if I was really going to like it, but then Stella, the seamstress, came to stay for two weeks, and the machine was whirring away all day turning out dresses and petticoats. I had to stand and be patient while things were cut and pinned and my figure drove Mother to despair. I wore something called a Ferris waist, a sort of bodice made of stiff cambric and buttons which certainly "did nothing" for me. But finally with the aid of fichus and ruffles and pleats, the lumps and protuberances and the heavy shoulder straps and buttons of the Ferris waist were almost hidden. Miss L. had said that, unless there was a large dinner party, Anna and I were to come down to dinner every night and, of course, we had to be "dressed." Stella made three delicious dresses for the evening, one in particular that I shall never forget. It had a pink taffeta slip and an overdress of white dotted

Here it's a better match. Perhaps the footman has given out quite a lot of punch.

net, with a ruffled fichu and a wide pink sash. I had never had such a trousseau and felt dizzy with excitement just looking at the dresses hung up around the sewing room. Granny came over to inspect my wardrobe and gave it her approval and, at the same time, handed me $10 to be given to the servants ($5 to the butler, $5 to the personal maid) at Miss L.'s when I left.

While all this made me feel tremendously important and Grown-up, when the train slid out of the station and the family's familiar faces vanished, I felt very small and lonely, and faced the next two weeks with trepidation. I took my sandwich out and started to munch it, and the porter brought me a glass of water. I kept my face turned resolutely toward the window, watching the drab landscape with unseeing eyes except when we passed Torresdale outside of Philadelphia and I saw the Convent of the Sacred Heart, where Mother had gone to school. The reason for my aloofness from my fellow passengers was that I had had very strict instructions from Granny and Mother. There were, apparently, kind-faced ladies and gentlemen who haunted trains and stations and who, though they seemed nice, were really terrible people. They would whisk you away at the drop of a hat and lock you in a small room where something terrible would happen to you. Even if your family were able to find you, you would never be the same after this weird experience. There had been a young lady called Dorothy Arnold who had been snatched away and was never heard of again. Granny shook her head and looked very severe when she told me about all this. "If Margaret [Miss L.'s personal maid] is not there to meet you," she said, "go directly to a policeman and ask him to take you to the stationmaster and then wait in the stationmaster's office until someone you *know* comes for you." "Yes, Granny," I had said, not listening very attentively, as I was gloating over all my new dresses. But now, when the gentleman across the aisle smiled and said, "I am taking a copy of *St. Nicholas* home to my niece, would you like to look at it?" I had uttered a cold "No, thank you" and pressed my nose to the windowpane. Was this one of those queer people Granny had warned against?

At last the five hours were over and the train pulled into Pennsylvania Station. The train porter, who had been tipped by Father, took my bags and put me in charge of a redcap. "Someone meeting you, Miss?" said the redcap ingratiatingly. "Yes," I said, the pulse beating wildly in my throat. Suppose no one was there, suppose the policeman I asked wasn't really a policeman but one of *those people* in disguise? Would I end up locked in a little room with probably not even a window in it? Looking wildly about me, I saw *not* Margaret but Anna and Miss Stringfellow. My joy and relief knew no bounds as I threw myself into their arms. Soon we were hustled into the motorcar and on our way to Maillard's for hot chocolate and buttered crumpets before going out to Long Island.

Anna's house was patterned on the English Tudor style. One entered the grounds past a little red brick gatehouse with leaded casement windows and then drove along a driveway edged with huge rhododendrons. The L.'s were Scottish and everything about the place was reminiscent of England or Scotland. The rooms were rather dark, mostly paneled, with casement windows, and window seats covered with cushions. The hall was all dark oak, with a huge table covered with English periodicals and beside it a great gong, which a footman sounded for dressing and for meals. It was like life in Peking in a way—or perhaps it was just like Trollope, whom I was starting to read. But anyway it suited me and I loved wandering past the beautiful herbaceous borders carrying the flower basket for Miss L., or driving along the winding roads in the wicker pony cart with Anna and Miss Stringfellow. It was idyllic and I reveled in it, until one night when Anna came to my room with a book. It was after eleven, and we were supposed to be asleep. I was startled when I heard a creak, and quickly turned on the light. Anna was standing in the middle of the room in her pink-and-white-striped wrapper, with a book in her hand.

A Windy Day

"Move over," she said as she got into bed. "I've got something to show you."

I had never noticed Anna reading and was rather surprised. "What is it?" I whispered.

"I found this book hidden away in a drawer in the attic," she said. "And I don't know whom it belongs to. But it's lots of fun."

"Yes," I said, "but what is it about?"

"Oh, it's marvelous," she sighed. "It's all about men and women and what they do and how they do it. Look," and she showed me a picture of a very strange thing.

I gave it a quick look. "How awful," I breathed. "What's that?"

Anna giggled. "You silly, it's a man." Her giggling began to get the best of her and she laughed and laughed. "Look at this," she said, pushing the book in front of my eyes. "Look what they are doing here."

But after a quick look, I astonished both her and myself by bursting into tears. I turned away and buried my face in the pillow. "No," I sobbed, "take it away. I don't want to see it. It's horrid."

"Don't be silly," said Anna. "Don't you want to learn? Don't you want to know what the Grown-ups do? This is what your father and mother do. This is what kissing means."

I turned and pushed her violently out of bed. "No," I cried, "no, not *my* father and mother. And kissing isn't like that either. Go away!"

"You are terribly silly," said Anna. "You are acting like a baby. You say you want boys to kiss you, you are always talking about it, and now you ought to know what it is all about. After all, you are thirteen."

I beat the pillow with my fists. "I shall never, never kiss anyone again," I almost shouted, "as long as I live. I don't want to know all about these horrid things. I hate everything in that disgusting book!"

The Concert Singer

"Well, you really *are* a baby," said Anna, getting up from the floor. "I thought we could have some fun looking at it, but I see you are just a ridiculous infant."

She went out and closed the door and I lay in the darkness, my eyes closed tight, trying to blot out the dreadful images that rose before them. The hot tears trickled down my face, and I licked them with my tongue as they fell. How salty they were! If being Grown-up meant such terrible things, I wanted to stay a child forever. Were Grown-ups really monsters when left alone? Did kissing a boy, which was fun, really end up in something so frightening, and did boys grow up to look like that picture? These and other thoughts kept me awake until almost dawn, and the lovely house and beautiful garden when I saw them the next day seemed haunted by an evil spirit. Anna never brought the subject up again, and I felt that she was contemptuous of me. And when I glibly quoted "the lilies and languors of virtue, the roses and raptures of vice," she laughed loudly and said, "Keep quiet, you don't know what you are talking about." I tried to look smug but realized I was on treacherous ground. What *did* those words really mean? I liked the sound but they didn't really make sense.

"You are an idiot," said Anna, and from then until the end of the visit I remained cowed before her, only showing off and enjoying myself under the kindly eyes of the Grown-ups. I put the Grown-ups back mentally where I had always imagined them—fully dressed and sitting up straight in chairs in a drawing room, making polite and interesting conversation.

Private Diary Belonging to Brooke Russell
Washington, D.C., 1915

Dedicated to H.L. R.D. C.A.

Author's note: When I moved back to Washington, D.C., it was important for me to have friends and soon I had a little clique. This diary was written between the ages of twelve and fourteen while I lived on DeSales Street.

Sunday, January 31, 1915 In the early morning it snowed, but later on it rained. I saw Dick at Sunday School. He is a pill! Oh I hate Sunday so. It is such a hypocritical sort of day. I wonder whether to-morrow will be an exciting day or not? I hope it freezes so that I can skate. Oh I hope it will be an interesting day.

Monday, February 1, 1915 This morning I had to stay in, as it was raining pitchforks. Drew lovely pictures, and tacked them on the wall. In the afternoon I went to the Ward's, as it was a theatrical meeting. They want to give a few stories in "Arabian Nights." Then I went to Zilla's for supper, and we drew Valentine's. Zilla is a dear. I love her. All afternoon I painted, and read. Mother was awfully irritable at dinner to-night. She said "Children are Hell!" I am afraid she does not believe in "Les jeunes innocents." I am horribly cynical, but I don't really mean to be. I suppose it is the feeling that I am not wanted, a sort of hunted animal affair, standing up for my own rights, that makes me such. Oh, if only

Mother would pet me a little more, but if I asked her to, I am afraid she would say "Now run along and play, don't be silly of course I love you." I know she does but she loves by fits and starts. I suppose it is because she has a temperament. This is all a pose, because I really know I am a spoiled child with everything I want. The world is a pose. Anyway, nothing is really natural. Oh la la. I wonder what will happen tomorrow.

Wednesday, February 3, 1915 In the evening Mother began reading "Don Quixote" it is awfully funny, but I feel so sorry for poor Don Quixote. He is crazy, you know, dear diary, quite crazy.

Thursday, February 4, 1915 No new fancies, dear diary—ah! But I forgot the "Sign of the Secret Ones." It is a new secret society which I made up you know, by which one communicates entirely by signs with the other members, that is in public, in private one may talk. . . . This afternoon I went to the Band of Mercy meeting at Helen's house. I am to play a fortune-teller. A charming Signorina, n'est-ce-pas? Do you think I look the part, not I! Oh la la! . . . I have written nothing interesting. The weather is continually horrid. I think that is the proper way to talk in a diary. Is it not? I went to see Miss Annie to-day, and am going to take music lessons from her hereafter. Our furnace man got drunk to-day. That forms an interesting episode in our domestic life. Good-night dear diary, fare thee well until to-morrow night, when again I shall unburden my soul to you.

Monday, February 8, 1915 . . . This afternoon I stayed home, and drew beautiful paper-dolls, which I am dying to sell, but I am afraid I cannot. Oh don't say that! You haven't seen them yet! Mother and Father went to a fancy dress-ball and dinner to-night. Mother went as a folly. Father as a Pierrot. Oh he was so cute! Dearest diary, don't you hope something nice will happen tomorrow? I am very rich as I have four car-tickets, and a dollar and a quarter. Dear diary, please come out of these pages, and go on a spree with me. Will you? I thought so! Good-night, I will come visit you to-morrow.

Tuesday, February 9, 1915 . . . I came home and went out walking with Father. Oh he is adorable, dear diary. Oh, but you don't know him. . . .

Wednesday, February 10, 1915 Dear diary, . . . I wrote a lovely poem to-day entitled the "Cow-bells." Very charming don't you know. Good-night dearest diary, to-morrow evening I shall again come to your secluded nook in the hills. Farewell dear hermit I now leave these lovely surroundings; the meadows, hills, woods, flowers, and fairies, for 1703 De Sales St. Washington D.C. Good-night, dear. I shall come to-morrow at sunset!

Tuesday, February 16, 1915 This morning, dear diary, I went out walking with Mother. I bought two lovely pair of shoes. A pair of street pumps, and a pair of dancing pumps. I also bought a pair of gray spats to wear with my street pumps. I tell you! Dearest Unky has broken his arm. Isn't that awful? I should say so! This afternoon I went to the movies with Evie and Zilla. We went to Grandalls, and another one too. We saw an awfully sad piece, which made me cry. It was called "A or the Daughters of The People." Oh it was triste to the last degree. Afterwards we walked joyfully into Hylers where we all had Sundaes. Good-night dear one. I will see you to-morrow.

Wednesday, February 17, 1915 Dear one, I had a wonderful time at the Manns. The adorable Dick was there. You remember that I told you that he asked Florence to kiss him. Well, at the Manns I said to him "You know, Nicky is a sweet dog, he doesn't go around and ask every girl he meets to kiss him, as some of them do!" Dick laughed, and said I was cute. He also said I was pretty, but I suppose he says that to every girl he meets. Oh dear, *do* you think I am pretty—medium colored hair, green eyes, pink cheeks, and a dimple, you musn't forget that! I think I have two. I must own that I did look nice in that enormous yellow paper hat, that I got as a cotillion favour. Dick gave me a parasol, and I gave him a cane. He had on a gray Norfolk suit, and looked awfully nice or rather simply ravishing. *Why,* did I tear up his photograph? Henry took me to supper, although Claude had engaged me. I was very glad to go with Henry. He said "You look as if you wanted something to feed upon" so I said "I do!" … P.S. Dick calls me "Tootsie" or "Boots." Sweet isn't it? Bah! I hate him only he serves to pass the time.

Dearest diary, I have not written for perfect ages, have I? A great change has come upon me because I have transferred my lavish affections from R.D. to H.L. (I do not use names for I never know into whose hands these pages may fall.) Perhaps it was H.L.'s smile that first attracted me. It is really *too* angelic is this smile. Next it is the eyebrows which curve upwards in the most wonderful way. Last but not least is the sweet way he behaves towards his mother. That always did attract me in a boy. Because most boys think it silly when it is not at all, for grown men are perfectly sweet with their mother's. The more you love your mother the more manly you are. Not slushy of course, but just nice, sweet, and respectful. Really I have waxed quite eloquent have I not, dear diary? … I suppose it is very wicked but I really wish someone would try and kiss me. It would be such fun! Of course, I would have to slap them, and say I would never speak to them again, but it would be fun just the same. Oh dear, I am dreadful, I hope nobody does try. It is not very likely I don't think!

Everybody thinks they understand me but no-body does. I'm really very unhappy. Mother is so moody. One minute she is cross or sarcastic, which is worse, and the next minute she is all smiles and expects me to be smily too. She just insults me! If I were to tell her that she would say, "What do brats of your age no [sic] about insulting," or something like that. I hate

to be called a brat, because I am not one. I am always good, I don't run after the boys, I don't chew gum, I don't talk slang. I don't go into a drug store alone, "shout or sing in the house," "Cry in public," etc. etc. Such is life. It doesn't pay to be good! … Mother is always saying that I think it is romantic to be misunderstood. I don't think it's romantic. But she doesn't understand me if she did she wouldn't quarrel with me. Father understands me like a book. He doesn't say anything when I get angry so immediately I relent and kiss him. Perhaps I love him more than Mother, I don't know, but I think not. I would like to show this to Mother, perhaps it would help her. But I am afraid she would begin to pity me, and then I would cry…. Grown up people can show off too. And when Mother calls me a brat, she is showing off. I would not show this to her nor anyone else for the world. It is too much my private feelings…. I suppose I shall read this some day when I am grown up, then I shall laugh and say, "What a brat, I was to be sure." But I don't feel like a brat, nor look like a brat, nor behave like a brat. So I can't possibly be one. Good-bye! Mother just said "What on earth have you got to have the blues about" Whew! Now she is preaching about me saying how well off I am. I lead a dog's life!

I am full of passion, of great feeling.

Is it not bad it is wasted?

"On what," you ask

"Flowers, music and self, self, self" I return

"Ah," you sigh

Beneath the willow tree.

Chapter 14

Morton

I fought desperately against growing up. I liked my position as a child who, from the sidelines, observed the Grown-up world. I did not want to enter the lists myself. Nature, unfortunately, was against me. I grew into a bouncing girl, well rounded and mature-looking, when I longed to be an ethereal, disembodied spirit. I read voraciously anything that came to hand. I wrote great reams of melancholy poetry and complicated novels. On the surface I was a well-brought-up, rather mousy adolescent, but underneath I longed to be an actress or something equally spectacular. I even toyed with the thought of becoming a nun. I began to feel that there was a door that had not yet opened for me—that there was something mysterious and delicious that could come from association with boys. The ones I knew, however, a year or two older than myself, were so dull (and what I privately called earthbound) that I had absolutely no means of communication with them.

Then I met Morton.

He was the older brother of one of my best friends and was nineteen to my fourteen. I heard about him first when his sister came over to spend the afternoon. We were acting *Alice in Wonderland.* She was Alice and I was the Duchess and we were discussing our parts when she told me that her brother had been asked to leave Yale and was home for the winter. "He behaved terribly," she said. "Mother is furious." (Her father was dead.)

"What did he do?" I asked, always interested in the out-of-the-way.

"Oh, dreadful things," she answered. "Drinking and running around with terrible girls. I don't know exactly but I think he is wonderful and it's nice to have him home. He is going to tutor here until the spring and then they may take him back."

We did not speak of him again, but the idea of Morton was planted in my mind—a Grown-up, rather wicked character.

Several days later a rehearsal of *Alice,* which was to be given for the Band of Mercy, was held at my friend's house, which was large, old-fashioned, and square, partly red brick, partly brownstone, and stood on a corner of one of Washington's big avenues. The drawing room was a fine place for rehearsal and we had great fun. I loved my part as I had to sing:

> Speak roughly to your little boy
> And beat him when he sneezes,
> He only does it to annoy
> Because he knows it teases.
> Wow, Wow, Wow.

After the rehearsal we had chocolate and cookies in the dining room and were having a high old time, wolfing down everything in sight, giggling like geese, when Morton suddenly appeared in the doorway. My friend ran up to him. "This is my brother, Morton," she cried, and she began to introduce us.

I could hardly believe my eyes. Not since Johnny Malone, the bugler in Peking, had I seen anything so beautiful. He gave us a lazy smile and sauntered slowly into the room. My heart skipped a beat when my friend said, "And this is Brooke." I scarcely dared to raise my eyes to his face but I noticed a book in his hand—*Plato and Platonism,* by Walter Pater, the book Mother had given me as a confirmation present. What luck!

"Do you like that book?" I demanded boldly, the blood rushing to my cheeks. "I've read it."

He looked at me and smiled. "Yes, I do," he answered, "but I prefer straight Plato." Well, this was almost too much for me. Someone young, beautiful, not a girl or a Grown-up, who liked to read! I went home with my head in the clouds and never heard a word that Catherine, who had come to fetch me, said to me.

That night in bed I revolved in my mind all the things I liked about him: his large, dark eyes all smudged about the sides as if they had been put in his head with dirty fingers; his gay, charming smile; his slow movements; the daring cigarette dangling from his mouth—heavens, it made my brain reel!

I managed to become more and more intimate with my friend and was constantly in and out of her house. But Morton was not often there and I only got glimpses of him going up the

Morton Hoyt, the brother of Eleanor Wylie the poetess, and of my friend Nancy Hoyt, who also became an author

Spring

—age fifteen

Spring is here
I see it in the mellow
* sunshine*
In the budding boughs
The crocuses are out
The birds are singing
A sweet fresh perfume
* pervades the air*
I am glad the winter is gone!

It was night, on a sandswept
* shore*
The waves were lapping
* lazily against the*
* steadfast rocks*
And I was alone!
Somewhere out of the dark-
* ness, a voice called*
—I glanced around—
I knew not what it was—

(continued on next page)

stairs to his room or moving along the dark hallway. One day, though, a glorious thing happened.

I was walking through Dupont Circle on my way home from school when I saw Morton coming toward me. I wanted to scuttle away into the bushes, as I realized that I would have to meet him face to face. But there he was, moving in that pantherlike way of his, his brown eyes sparkling! "Hello, Brooke," he said, "it's nice to see you." I was covered with confusion and was unable to answer. It seemed incredible that this godlike creature could remember my name. He motioned to a park bench. "Can't you sit down and talk a moment?" he asked. "It's nice to see you away from that giggling horde that you're usually with."

I gave Catherine a look; she was glaring at me. I smiled sweetly and said in my best French that my friend's brother had something to tell me and would she sit on the next bench, please. She shrugged her shoulders and rolled her eyes, but went over and sat down, determinedly turned in our direction.

Morton had *The Frogs* by Aristophanes in his hand and I started to question him about it. It was in English, but he pulled a Greek version out of his pocket and explained to me what fun it was to read the two at the same time. "It's a very funny play," he said. "And, even though it's extremely well translated, it seems to me that a few points have been lost here and there. Listen to this." And he gave me a line or two from the English, then *his* version from the Greek.

I was way out over my depth, but not since I had first learned to spell had such an exciting thing happened to me. This was not a Grown-up talking down to me, showing off his own knowledge, or a boy my own age who always had me tongue-tied. Here, at last, was someone taking for granted that I knew a thing or two and treating me as an equal. I could have stayed on that park bench forever. Catherine, though, had other ideas and finally came over.

"You have your homework to do," she said, "and your maman would not like you to stay here talking."

I longed to implore her to let me stay but I did not want to appear too childish. Morton solved it by sticking his books in his pockets and getting up. "It's been fun," he said. "Let's meet again."—Meet again, what magic words!

From then on I haunted Dupont Circle, but it was not often that I found him. His habits were erratic and so was his reading, as I soon became aware. I constantly nagged Mother to let me take Greek lessons. She could not understand this sudden passion for study and, I think, felt that Walter Pater and Santayana and Vorticism had become a boomerang. I heard her complaining to her friend Lucretia, "I am going to have to take Brooke out of Miss Madeira's. They are turning her into a bluestocking. She wants to learn Greek!"

"Ah, the thirst for knowledge in youth is a very touching thing," murmured Lucretia, who was a rather intense character and, I felt, a poor influence on Mother.

"I can't understand it," said Mother thoughtfully, "there must be some special reason behind all this."

I got up and shut my door and returned to the poem I was writing. It was blank verse, all about love and unhappiness and useless searching.

I wrote poems from morning to night and lay about the house on the floor with my feet up on a chair, or across the bed with my head hanging down, or sprawled on a sofa. I could not seem to sit up straight or do anything in a normal way. It drove Mother mad. Things were difficult for us anyway. Father was away in Mexico and Mother and I were alone together. She was having an even gayer time than when Father was with us and, as usual, I was a disappointment to her. Instead of being the nice, meek, cheerful child she wanted, I did nothing but sigh and moan or laugh hysterically and turn up my nose at her friends.

"You are not trying to be rude, are you?" Mother would say with a stamp of her foot when I had been particularly objectionable. "Because I simply will not tolerate it." My answer

*Then it called again, low
     and clear there in the
     heavy blackness of the
     night
My heart leapt within me at
     the sound
I understood
It was the call of a kindred
     soul
Somewhere far out in the
     night, across the shim-
     mering sea
Standing on a shore, far
     away in an eternal
     land—
A voice called
I heard and understood
Some day we shall meet
Somewhere, I know not how
But my soul is glad, for I
     know I am not alone
I know that far off in the
     oblivious universe
One waits who understands!!*

POEM

—age fifteen

Oh I am happy
I wish to sing
To tell the world of my joy
To say that I am young, and
*   the world is full of sun-*
*   shine*
Soft, mellow sunshine, shin-
*   ning on a bed of flowers*
Night may come, but I care
*   not*
I live in the rapture of the
*   moment*
The wonderful, golden
*   moment.*
Why should I think of night
And the chilling dew?
My life is like a golden cup
Filled to the brim with
*   nectar*
My soul has been wrapt the
*   whole long winter*
In a mantel of sleep
But now t'is awakening with-
*   in me*
Fluttering, and whispering
*   within me*
Singing a song tourquoise
*   skips*
And sunkiss'd flowers.
"Awake, awake," it sings so
*   softly*
And see the wondrous things
*   about you*

was to give what I felt was a cryptic smile and float out of the room. It was enough to try the temper of the most angelic parent.

Then something happened that drew us very close together. One morning we heard a man running down our street calling out: "Extra, extra! All about the incident in Mexico!" We pricked up our ears, thinking immediately of Father, and Mother sent the maid out to buy the paper. Upon reading the headlines, we burst into tears. It was all about Father! He and his Marines were guarding the waterworks at El Tajin and a demand had been made that the waterworks be surrendered. Father and the opposing Mexican officer met under a flag of truce to discuss it. As Father went out on foot, the Mexican rode up insolently on his horse. He demanded that the waterworks be surrendered at once. Father said, "Go to hell!" and turned back, fully expecting a bullet to be put into him. The waterworks were held and Father came out of it a hero.

Grandfather and Grandmother came around at once and we dined with them that night. Grandfather had American flags everywhere in the dining room, including small ones stuck into the wine jelly and ice cream. When he stood up and proposed a toast to Father, Uncle Charlie and Granny and Mother and I all stood up, too, and cried a bit. It was a wonderful evening.

That night I took a long time saying my prayers, begging God to forgive me for having been thinking only of myself when darling Father was in danger. I was very chastened and Mother was quiet, too. After that we spent more time at home together, reading aloud and talking about Father and reading and rereading his letters. But then we got caught up again in our life. Mother started going out with her friends and I started dragging Catherine back to Dupont Circle.

After a few unsuccessful sorties I saw Morton one day lolling on the park bench, reading *Anna Karenina*. We met often after that and went from *Anna Karenina* to *The Idiot* and then to Chekhov's short stories. This was pretty heady stuff, particularly when read to me by Morton, his smudgy eyelids half-closed, his long lashes sweeping his cheek. I hardly dared to breathe, for fear that I would break the spell. At home, I wrote furiously and, influenced by the Russians, my poems and stories concentrated more and more on the intricacies of the soul. I had a marvelous time steeping myself in gloom. The days were recorded in my diary as being of different colors. It all depended on whether I saw Morton or not. Rosy, pink, or gold, when I saw him—or gray and drab when there was no glimpse.

One day is recorded as being black, black, black. That day I was walking joyfully through Dupont Circle, with Catherine at my heels, when a revolting sight met my eyes. There was Morton, sitting on the grass with another young man and two frightfully common girls, called in the slang of that day "chippies." And what were they doing? Reading poetry? No, horrible, horrible sight—all four were eating bananas! I was shaken to the core and hurried away, hoping that I had not been seen, although Catherine's laughter as she followed me was loud enough to wake the dead. I tore up quite a few poems on my return and did not go near Dupont Circle for a week.

The week was just ending when Morton called me on the telephone. He wanted to know if he could come to see me. It was getting colder and the park bench was not as sheltered as one would want. Mother would not let a boy come alone to see me; there always had to be two or more boys at a time and another girl, with Catherine close by. As I had never wanted to be alone with a boy before, the ruling had not bothered me. But now I wanted desperately to be alone with Morton. How to arrange it?

Mother was downstairs and I was afraid she would hear me, so I mumbled into the telephone—Morton was telephoning from a booth somewhere, judging by the background noises—and he could not apparently understand a word I said. "Telephone tomorrow same time," I hissed. "I can't talk now."

"All right," he answered, and hung up.

The human faces, sad, and laughing
Tearful, smiling, dazed and wondering
All about you.
No, you are indeed not different
Each and every is the same
Each one knows a loving person
Waiting, watching for his return
Each one has a world of thoughts
Revolving, forming in the mind;
Come, awake unfold this mantel
Wrapt about your sleeping soul,
Take it off and cast it from you
So, that you may see aright
Ah, awake and be more kindly
Be more lenient towards this mass
And stepping off your self-made pedestal
Walk in friendship thru' the throng

The Real Sportswoman

POEM

—age fifteen

*To-day I feel gloomy and
    moody
And my thoughts are like
    thunder-clouds
Rolling and rumbling about
    me
Enveloping me in their
    blackness
They press ever closer about
    me
And weigh down my spirit
    with lead
Yet I love their congenial
    blackness
And find comfort in being so
    sad.*

I sat down absolutely limp with emotion. The fact that he was telephoning from a booth seemed incredibly romantic and significant. He obviously did not want his family to know. It was a secret thing between us. I adored secrets and was constantly inventing new languages in which to communicate with my friends, and I liked to lock things in strongboxes with alarms on them. But this secret, a telephone call from Morton that no one else knew about, was the biggest secret I had ever had! I sat for a moment wondering how to arrange this heavenly meeting. Then I went downstairs to the drawing room.

Mother and her friends, Lucretia and Clara, were sitting at the tea table, drinking pale jasmine tea and smoking cigarettes in long holders. "It is a tear of vice on the cheek of affluence," Lucretia was saying as I came in. Then she stopped and they all looked at me. I shook hands and made my curtsy, then sat down.

"Have you finished your homework?" said Mother brightly.

"Yes, Mother," I answered meekly. I had not even looked at it, but I wanted to keep her in a good humor.

The conversation seemed to dry up with my appearance and, in a few moments, Clara began to draw on her gloves. "I must go," she announced. I followed her to the door. She was my favorite of all Mother's friends. She was extremely beautiful, with golden hair and large, blue-green eyes and had a lovely, slender figure. I had gleaned that in her girlhood there had been an unhappy love affair with a married man, and out of grief when her lover forsook her she chose to lead a semiretired life. It was for this reason that she never wore colors but dressed always in black or gray. To me she was like one of the ladies of King Arthur's court; I admired her stand immensely in regard to mourning a love. She was also the only one of Mother's friends who took me and my struggle to become a writer seriously. In fact, I felt so close to her that I had already confided to her my admiration for Morton. Now I seized my opportunity to speak to her alone.

"Miss E.," I said, "Morton called me just now."

"Did he?" she said, opening the front door. "What's he up to now?"

I followed her onto the porch. "He wants to call on me," I whispered hoarsely, "but how can I do it?"

"Why not?" she said, stopping and looking at me. "I don't believe your mother will like him, but if you have a little tea party she probably won't mind."

"Oh, but that's just it!" I exclaimed, seizing her hand. "I don't want to have a tea party. I want to be alone with him."

Miss E. laughed. "Whatever for?" she said. "Can't you two talk with other people about?" She looked at me quizzically.

I shook my head. "No," I said, "it's not the way we like to talk, and besides, I have a very special reason for wanting to be alone."

By this time we had reached the little iron gate to our garden and Miss E. paused. "Tell me, what do you want to do?" she asked. Fortunately, it was almost dark, so she could not see how red my cheeks grew.

"I want to read him my poems," I said.

Miss E. nodded. "I see," she said.

"Won't you help me?" I asked. "Won't you ask Mother to do something with you the day after tomorrow and keep her out, say, from four to six? Then he could come here."

She shook her head. "No, I couldn't," she said.

I threw my arms around her neck. "Oh, please, please, Miss E. You are the only person who really understands me. Won't you help me? If you only knew Morton, I know that you would feel as I do. Dear, dear Miss E.—*please*."

I looked searchingly into her face and she smiled. "It's a dreadful thing to do to Mabel," she said. "If she should find out she would never speak to me again and I wouldn't blame her, but I'll do it. However, mind you, stick to reading poems and don't get silly."

I knew what she meant and was shocked. "Oh, I promise, darling Miss E., cross my heart and hope to die." She gave me a kiss and went off.

POEM

—*age fifteen*

There is a storm without
The great black clouds cover
    the sky
And the thunder shakes the
    very earth
Lightening, the tourch of
    heaven
Comes in quick, clear flashes
And the rain beats against
    the windows
O, I love it
And my spirit dances with
    joy.
A chord in my soul
That I knew not I had
Has been struck
And my whole being
Is vibrating in response
I feel like a Pagan
On a feast day
Wild, barbaric,
Who says we're a civilized
    people
Down in our hearts we are
    always the same

POEM*

—age fifteen

Oh, God, I was happy once
And my soul hung on a silver
*   thread*
I throbbed and thrilled with
*   eagerness*
As I raised to my lips the fair
*   cup of happiness*
I saw the sun and the pale
*   moon glitter*
Into the heart of my golden cup.
Whilst the rose petals
*   swirling o'er its surface*
In toxicated me with their
*   fragrance.*
Fool, t'was but a soap-bubble
That burst in the light of day
That vanished into the hot,
*   hot air*
At the dawn of the garish day
My cup it was madly torn
*   from me*
And dashed on the hard, bare
*   ground*
I wept like a child, then
*   smiled*
Yes, smiled at the man who
*   broke it*
But the pain in my heart is
*   burning*
Burning me slowly away
Yet I shall smile at the man
*   who broke it*
Yes, smile to my dying day!

*This one drew *very* sarcastic comments from Mother.

As I walked past the drawing-room door I heard Lucretia saying, "A Vorticist is always in the center of a Vortex."

Miss E. kept her promise. She invited Mother to go to some special exhibition at the Corcoran Gallery and then to have tea afterward. It was arranged that Morton was to come at four, and from three on I was in a fever of excitement. I examined myself critically in the glass. What I saw did not reassure me. I had a turned-up nose, round pink cheeks, gray-green eyes, and a long braid of mouse-colored hair. I had on a white silk blouse and a blue pleated serge skirt. There was nothing glamorous about me. I longed for flowing chiffon and sables and a long, gold cigarette holder. I sat down in front of the mirror and tried different expressions. Did I look prettier with my mouth open laughing, or with just a subtle lopsided smile? Should I look down and then up quickly, or was it better to do it slowly? I studied myself for so long that I began to grow tired and started to make faces as I used to do when I was younger. I realized that no good could come of these grotesqueries and so concentrated again on my costume. I took off my infinitesimal string of pearls and got out from my bureau drawer a carved piece of jade that Prince W. had given me in Peking, which was on a black ribbon that I could wear around my neck. I tried it on and liked it better than the pearls, even though it went right down the middle of my chest and seemed to draw attention to my sprouting bosom. I absolutely hated *that,* and was about to take off the jade when the bell rang. I had one more thing to do and so rushed down to Mother's room just as I was. On Mother's dressing table stood her lily-of-the-valley perfume and I put some behind my ears and along my hairline and on my eyelids, as I had seen Mother do. Thus fortified, I descended the stairs.

Eliza was waiting at the bottom of the stairs.

"Young gemman to see you," she said.

"Oh," I said. "Well, bring in some tea, will you, please?" I had not dared to order tea as I wanted Morton's visit to seem unpremeditated.

Eliza gave me a sour look. "The cook's out," she said.

"Well, surely you can fix up tea for two?" I said in a grave manner and then, as she still hesitated, I played my trump card. "I'll give you two dollars," I whispered. She smiled, her white teeth shining in her black face, and went off to the dining room.

I skipped gaily into the drawing room—all plans for slinking in like Theda Bara forgotten. "Oh, Morton," I cried, "this is wonderful. I'm so glad you could come."

"I'm glad, too," he said, giving my hand a squeeze. "I haven't seen you for ages. You look awfully pretty today."

This was a terrific start to the visit. Where could we go from here? A compliment such as that should have been the climax. I was afraid that the visit might be a flop from then on.

We sat down on the sofa and Morton began to talk. Unlike our other talks, when we spoke mostly of books, this time he wanted to talk about himself. He was unhappy, life was not treating him right, time was passing by, and he was not getting anywhere. He was disgusted with himself. Eliza brought in the tea, and I asked her to shut the door as she went out. I felt that Morton was really going to confide in me, and he did. He seemed quite wound up. He hated Washington, he said, there was nothing for him to do there. His older sister, who was a well-known poetess and lived in the South of France, had asked him to come and visit her. He wanted to do that but his mother would not let him. He felt he had talents that had been given no scope.

"Great heavens!" he cried. "Think what I could do if I could get to Greece, or even Turkey. I might swim the Hellespont, I might write like Byron. At least I would be heard from—I would not die of dry rot."

I sighed deeply. These, too, were my feelings. Here was I, at fourteen, keen to live and take part in things and I also was dying of dry rot.

Morton looked at me as he lit another cigarette. "You may not know it," he said, "but you have been the only real interest I have had in Washington. Your interest in reading and your intellectual curiosity have been manna to me."

POEM

—about age fifteen

Will I always be an atom
A pulse in the wide beating
    world
A grain of ash
That slowly drops
From the altar of God
Is there nothing more
In the cup of Fate
But a tasteless, colorless
    draught,
Where ever I go
Whatever I do
Will it always be unknown?
O, God give me the power
The will, the strength, the
    force,
To be cast in relief on the
    bronze wall
In the soft putty of human
    existance
Let me get what I want
    when I want it,
Let me get it and keep it—
    my own
Let me live, wild and free
Yet with a face that is all my
    own
This drabness
This sereness
Is ghastly.

*T'was but last night I had a
vision
That a man borne down
with years
Sad, and marked, and worn
with longing
Came unto me and said:
"O, foolish one so wildly saying
That God has passed thee by,
That thy life is empty
That for thee the flowers soon
die
And that thy gold soon turns
to dust.
Knowest thou not, O unbe-
liever
That every nut its kernel
hath,
That every soil hath flowers
That every rock its share of
gold?
T'is thou who art the empty
shell
The gold that turns to barren
dust
Awake! Arise! O useless idler
Take thy spade and take
thine ax
Go forth and make thy soil
fertile
Make the flowers bloom for
thee."
He passed away: and I,
stirred to my soul,
Slept not.*

I could hardly contain myself. I felt that, now or never, it was my moment to act. "Morton," I said, "you have read so much, you know so much, your taste in reading is so wonderful, would you mind if I read you some of my poems?"

He flicked his ash carelessly onto the carpet, and I made a mental note to clean up later. "Go ahead," he said lazily, throwing himself back in the chair. "I'd love to hear them."

I pulled my copybook out from behind the sofa pillow where I had put it the moment Mother had left the house, and started. I chose one that I felt was our theme song:

> Will I always be a unit?
> A pulse in the wide, beating world,
> A grain of ash
> That slowly drops
> From the altar of God?
> Is there nothing more
> In the cup of Fate
> Save a tasteless, colorless draught?
> Wherever I go,
> Whatever I do,
> Will it always be unknown?
>
> O God, give me the power,
> The will, the strength, the force
> To be cast in relief on the bronze ball.
> In the soft putty of human existence.
> Let me get what I want when I want it.
> Let me get it and keep it my own.
> Let me be wild and free
> Yet with a law that is all my own.

I looked up when I had finished. "Do you like it?" I asked timidly, throwing back my horrid braid that had fallen over my shoulder.

He gave me one of his delicious lazy smiles. "Read more," he said, throwing his cigarette into the teacup.

Encouraged in this entrancing way, I read on and on—a little embarrassed sometimes by the things I had put down on paper (were they really me?). Anyway, I had written them and I was reading them to the most gloriously intelligent person I had ever met.

When I had done, Morton was silent for a while. Then, standing up, he pulled me to my feet and, putting his arms around me, kissed me on the mouth.

"Dear God," he said, "you *are* a remarkable child." And, as I wrote in my diary, "I almost swooned." The fact that he left at once was all the better. I could live and relive this wondrous experience. I forgot my promise to Miss E. One could never die of dry rot after having had such a wicked and exciting moment.

Washington Diary 1917

A watercolor taken from my Washington Diary

Author's note: I began to have romantic attachments at the age of fourteen. I was particularly fascinated by Morton Hoyt. Morton was slouchy and always had a cigarette hanging from his mouth, which I found appealing. He seemed so much older than the other boys I knew and I felt that through him I was stepping into grown-up life.

Everything I have written before has no meaning. I have met Morton. O, dear diary, I could not believe that such a person as Morton existed. He is *so* beautiful. His eyes look as though they had been put in with dirty fingers. Lovely blue and gray shadows all around them.

Mother hates Morton. She says that he is too

old for me—(He is 18) and that he has been kicked out of Yale and that he is a bad boy. She can't say too much because he is Nancy's brother, and she loves Nancy.

I went to Nancy's this afternoon. We are learning our parts for the Band of Mercy play. Morton was in the Library reading. Nancy says he reads all day.

Helen has a wonderful box. It is made of iron, and if you don't know how to open it, it rings a loud bell. She keeps it under her bed with her poems in it. O, I wish I had such a box. I feel sure some *cad* will find my diary.

I met Morton in DuPont Circle, he was sitting on a bench in the shade. I made Caterine sit on another bench, and went up and sat beside him. O dear diary, he is so *clever*. He says such wonderful things. I could listen to him forever. He reads nothing but Russian writers, Turgenev, Dostoievesky (?) Tolstoi. I must read them too. He told me that I was pretty. O, I hope he means it, because I know I'm not really pretty. I looked at myself a long time in the glass last night. I had to stop, because I felt I was going crazy. I couldn't believe that face was mine. I don't feel *inside,* the way I look *outside.* Which is real—my face, or me? O, I must stop. This is too much for me.

I can play the piano quite well now. I played "Poor Butterfly" and "Oh Johnny" right off from the notes. Mother wants me to take singing lessons, but I want to study greek. Morton is studying Greek with a teacher, and I could take lessons there too. I want to read Socrates and Plato, and "burning Sappho." Am reading Tolstoi.

Mother says it's all a pose, my wanting to study greek. She says I am getting terribly silly, and I bore her. Well, she bores me. Great heavens, can't I even want to improve my mind, without being told I'm silly. It's really too much. O, if only Morton could talk to Mother. He sits a lot in Dupont Circle, it's near his Greek professor. O, he is really divine. I think perhaps he is a little wicked too. They say he was drinking at Yale. I wonder if I like wicked people?

Evie's family have given her a car, and she can drive if the chauffeur is with her. She took Nancy and me out yesterday, and we had the top down, and went all the way down Connecticut Ave. and around the mall. It was heavenly. I had a new yellow hat, with dark blue flowers on it.

Louise gave a dance. It was great fun, and I would have had a good time, only Morton wasn't there. He said they were all too young for him. Dick and Henry, and Charlie and Billie were there of course, and Dick said "Why are you so snooty?" I laughed, but I *do* think they are all rather silly. They never read anything, or talk about anything interesting. How could I ever have liked them. O, it is so wonderful to know someone like Morton. Although when I am with him, I have to be careful, because I know so little. They had punch with "something" in it at Louise's, and Duer drank too much, and had to be taken home—out of the cradle and into the punch bowl!

I feel terribly sad to-day. I don't know why. I lay on the sofa and sang sad songs until Mother said for heaven's sakes stop. She was trying to rest, and I was driving her crazy. Then I went to my room, and leant out the window, and looked at the nuns walking in the convent garden. I think that I shall become a nun.

Have written a great many poems lately. Had lunch with Grandmother and Grandfather. Granny gave me a brooch of seed pearls and tourquoises. It is awfully pretty. Mother bought me a yellow chiffon party dress and bronze slippers.

Mother went to lunch with Senator S. and didn't get back until 6 o'clock. They drove to Mt. Vernon. What on earth do grown-ups find to talk about all day! We got a long letter from Father to-day. I let Nicky smell it, and I think that he knew it was from Father because he wagged his tail.

Went to Janet's for lunch. Her brother John was home from college. Janet and I were practicing new laughs, and he got furious. He said we were the silliest girls he'd ever seen. Janet fought with him, but I was upset. Am I silly, dear diary? O, heavens, if people would just let me alone, so I could do the things I really like. Study greek, and talk to Morton.

Bought a Ouija Board. Janet and Zilla and I played it. It said awfully strange things. Said I am going to marry very soon. [I did.] Will it be to Morton, I wonder. After the others left, I played it by myself, and it ran all over the place. It scared me. Was I doing it myself or is it a spirit?

O, dear diary, I hardly dare to write it. Mother was out, and Morton came to tea. I had it in the drawing room, just like Mother, and then I read all my poems to Morton, and O, dear diary, then he kissed me. O, to be kissed by Morton, clever, beautiful, wicked Morton. O, I just think of it over and over. I suppose I'm wicked, and I

suppose it was awful to let Morton kiss me, but dear diary, I'm fourteen years old, almost 15, and I'm not a child.

Have been reading about Sophie Arnould, an 18th century actress, because we have a picture of her. I think I'd like to be an actress. Saw Morton in duPont Circle. He was with some dreadful looking people, and much older.

Morton sent me a book, some short stories by Turgenev. I could hardly believe it. There it was on the hall table when I came home from school. It says to B. from M. O, I shall devour every word of it. How happy I am. Mother says I am too young to have presents, even books sent me, but Miss Emory was here, and she said "Why not? It's part of growing up." Growing-up!!! If they only knew how old I feel.

I live now just to see Morton, everything else, school, my friends, the family, all seem dim, and far away. The days are colored by whether I see him or not—gold, and rose, and green, like sunsets. The days I don't see him are gray and sad.

How I hate dancing class. The same dull old boys, so terribly silly and boring. I can't talk to them anymore. Charlie said "I hear that you are crazy about Morton," and I said "Who told you that?" and he said "A little bird, but seriously Brooke, he's just a bum, nobody ever asks him anywhere, he's terrible" and I said "He doesn't want to be bothered with people like you and me, Charlie." Charlie laughed and whistled, and I wanted to slap his silly pink face.

Morton's older sister is a famous poetess, and she ran off with a married man and lives in the south of France. Morton told me this to-day in duPont Circle. Caterine says she is going to tell Mother I see Morton, but I don't think she will. She likes him.

To-day I went to Nancy's and her mother called her, and Morton came out of his room and kissed me. O, dear God, how wonderful it was. I would like to die now. It's not like anything on heaven or earth how I feel. O, if Father and Mother knew I had let Morton kiss me. I know I am horrible, and I know God must be angry with me. How can I say my prayers to-night, but perhaps God will understand.

Mother says we are going down to Santo Domingo to join Father after my school is over. I long to see Father, and I know that he must be lonely without Mother and me, but O, I hate to leave Janet and Evie and Zilla and MORTON.

Miss Emory came to tea with Mother and she laughed and said "How are you going to be able to leave Morton, Brooke?" I was furious, because I had told Miss Emory privately how I felt, and to have her say that in front of Mother made me mad. You can't trust grown-ups. They all stick together. Mother laughed and said "She's like a love sick calf, and all over that perfectly useless boy. It's time she went away." *Useless.* Morton who speaks greek, and writes essays, and is so clever to talk to. It made me sick.

I went to Nancy's for lunch and Morton came in with a little black cap on his head to keep his hair down. I didn't like it. Morton is wonderful, but I think that is rather silly. Nancy says he goes out with chorus girls, and I saw him with a cheap looking girl the other day again. I know he's wicked, but when he talks to me of poetry and books, and thoughts, and says he'd like to kiss me—I don't care about anything.

It seems to me all my life I have been moving first one place then another. We are coming back next winter, but Mother says I am to go to boarding school, so it must be the same—and Morton, you ask. What about Morton. Ah, when I am very old, and read this, I will say, how absurd, I was only a child, perhaps I am, but I don't want to grow any older. I want to stay as I am, and love Morton as I do. He says I am a child, but that I have a wonderful mind, that he is too old for me, and too sophisticated, but then he kisses me—(not often, because we aren't alone much) and then he says I'm sweet, and it's too bad I'm not older. I shall never forget him.

Chapter 15

Saño Domingo

Lieutenants
and Caribbean
Moonlight

Mother would often sit for hours at tea talking with a gentleman. It had always seemed extraordinary to me that they could stay still for so long in one place and go droning on and on endlessly. Now that I had met Morton I began to understand the fascination of conversation with the opposite sex. Whenever I could I smuggled him into the house. I had to bribe Eliza to keep her quiet, but Catherine, in true French fashion, fell victim to a whiff of romance, so was no problem. It was a delicious winter and I walked on air. My appetite for knowledge was sharpened, as I wanted to astound Morton with my erudition. The Renaissance poets, Pushkin, Samuel Butler, Fielding, François Villon, Goethe's conversations with Eckermann, Stendhal, the de Goncourts—any book that Mother threw down I took up. At the same time I hung on to every word my English teacher at Miss Madeira's spoke and, with her, fed on the Brownings, Keats, Shelley, and Byron. Knowing I was no beauty, I wished to dazzle by my mind and spirit. It was hard work and I slept so badly that Mother had to call in a doctor and ask to have the clock on the public school nearby stopped.

I discovered that Morton wrote too—short essays on books and authors, comparative sketches, and bits of criticism. He would lie stretched out on our best sofa, his feet on a cushion, a cigarette dripping ashes onto the carpet, while I sat stiff on a chair, hardly daring to move lest I break the spell. We talked and read aloud for as long as I thought it safe. Then when I knew Mother would be returning soon, I would say, "I am dreadfully sorry, Morton, but you know what an old-fashioned dragon Mother is. She will be home any minute and you must go." He would get up in that almost somnambulistic and utterly captivating way of his and, after saying, "Ye gods, is it that late?" would give me a kiss. What glorious afternoons they were! The talk—the strange effect Morton had on me, making me feel that I had a little electric engine buzzing away inside me—and at the end the kiss!

Then came the bombshell. Father, who was in charge of the

Northern Province of Santo Domingo, wanted Mother and me to join him. Much as I loved my father, I was heartbroken. We were very busy packing up and having Stella make us summer dresses and saying good-bye to all our friends. Though I tried not to be sulky and cross, I had to give way occasionally by weeping on the shoulder of Mother's friend, Miss Clara E.

My house in Santiago de los Caballeros

"There, there, don't cry, Brooke," she said. "You will soon forget Morton."

"Never, never," I cried vehemently.

Miss E. smiled. "Oh, yes, you will. There are a lot of nice young second lieutenants in Santo Domingo."

"Ugh!" I said. "I am sure they are all dreadful. And I don't want to meet them."

Morton said he would be very lonely and gloomy without me, and he read some sad poetry. He held my hand as he read, which made it impossible for me to concentrate.

At last everything was packed. We spent our last night with Grandfather and Granny, then took the train to New York and boarded the ship for Santo Domingo. The trip down was horrible. The Panama Line, at that time, was run mostly for the convenience of the Canal people going back and forth to Panama, so very little attention was paid to comfort or cuisine. In eat-

At Miss Madeira's hearing something she doesn't like.

ing something called "diplomat's pudding," I found myself crunching on a cockroach, and the smell of old rope and tar and ancient soups hung over the ship like a cloud. We never smelled the fresh sea air. The passenger list was mainly composed of children, a great many of whom wore black underclothes so that the dirt would not offend one's eye. I took it all as a symbol of what life without Morton was going to be like. I had expected a dull, drab world and that was what I was getting.

When there was an earthquake the first night we arrived in Santiago, I stood in the doorway with Mother while Father told us what to do and glumly watched the pictures falling off the walls and the flower vases tumbling. As I wrote in my diary: "We had an earthquake the other night. The house rocked and creaked, but I was not afraid. I thought this would be a wretched hole. I expected no good of it. If I die an obscure death in an obscure place, well, such is the fate of some."

Santiago de los Caballeros actually was an enchanting little town. It was prettily situated on a bluff above the Yaque del Norte River amidst lovely trees. The houses were mostly one-story and were painted in pastel colors. The gardens were full of roses and bougainvillaea, and the two plazas where one walked in the evening and listened to band concerts were filled with flowering bushes and flowerbeds.

It was the custom for all the boys and young men to walk around the plaza in one direction, the girls in the other, so they always met face to face and could exchange glances. The older people watched from the benches to see that the glances were not too long and that trysts were not made.

There was a large group of second lieutenants stationed there—young men who had left Virginia Military Institute to join the Marines. They were fiery young Southerners and fell quickly into the habits of this tropical place. As I was the only young American girl, I was naturally much sought after. It was a new role for me and Mother encouraged it. We had thés dansants at our house once a week and danced continually from four to six to a small Marine orchestra. There was lemonade and iced tea and lots of small cakes with colored icing made by Harvey, our Marine chef. Mother joined in the dancing and so did some of the other wives of the officers and businessmen. Although I had many friends among the Dominican girls, they did not come to these parties because their customs were quite different. At the Dominican dances, a girl took the arm of her partner and paraded around the room for fifteen minutes or so while two rows of duennas, waving their fans languidly, watched from the sidelines.

Suddenly, for no reason at all, it seemed, I was allowed so much freedom that these sharply chaperoned girls could not keep up with me. I imagine that it was the war influence that broke Mother's up-to-now rigid rules. I think she felt sorry for all the young men who might, at any moment, be ordered overseas. They seemed very old to me, their ages ranging from twenty to twenty-six, and I almost always called them "Mister" in deference to their advanced years. Every day after my Spanish lesson with Mother, I went riding with two or three of them, and every evening we went to the band concert at the plazas, or the young officers gave parties, or we went to the Eden Café! The Eden Café had bushes around each table, which made it appear that one was in a little room of one's own. I drank lemonade and became an incorrigible flirt.

My romance with Morton had whetted my appetite for the opposite sex and, once started on these entrancing experiments, I could not stop. With Morton I had felt humble and overwhelmed by his superior wisdom and, to me, utter sophistication. But these young men, though older, were much less complex. They either had ideas of Southern chivalry or they were overawed by the commanding officer's daughter. Anyway, I found that I could do anything I liked with them and they took me quite seriously. I learned to look up, and then down, then look them straight in the eye as I asked some artless question. I heard them catch their breath as I leaned toward them in the

Father and Mother in Santiago, 1917

moonlight. Father and Mother really had no idea what I was up to. But then neither did I, really. In spite of all my reading I still thought that if a man kissed you very much a baby would eventually pop out of your tummy. But at just what point the kissing had to stop I was not sure. It was all very mysterious and quite fascinating. I was beginning to realize more than ever that the old saying "Boys don't really like girls like that" was completely wrong. Like a timid bather approaching the sea for the first time, I felt exhilarated from the water lapping about my feet, but was afraid to trust myself further.

The lieutenants were easy to keep in place. By Mother's insistence we always went in threes, and there were so many of them that it was rarely that I could slip away with one and exchange a light kiss. They were really very romantic in their uniforms, taking their turn at being officer of the day at the fort, riding out into "the bush" on patrol, and learning how to deal with the men under their care. They came to me with problems and hopes and ambitions and, looking back, I feel that they must have been exceptionally nice. I pretended in my diary that I was bored. I set myself up as quite an intellectual, too. Here is one bit:

"We went to the T.'s for dinner last night, and I was bored. After dinner, Mrs. T. started to play the piano. She plays with superb technique but no feeling. So, consequently, I was revolted. Then Mr. Doane asked me to go to the park. He told me that the last thing he heard when he left the Junior Officer's Quarters was instructions to take me to the park. We met Mr. Davis and Fugate and went to the Eden Café but I left soon because I didn't feel well. Besides, everything simply bored me to tears last night and I longed for soul communion with Morton." Of course, I was not bored a bit, I was having the time of my life!

One day, though, things took a different turn. We went to a reception and dance at the Santiago Club. The Dominican soprano Julietta Otera sang—Puccini, Verdi—and there were some piano solos and then dancing. We danced the currently popular Dominican dances, the danzón (a sort of cha-cha), the mazurka, the waltz, and the two-step. Each girl had a little program with a pencil attached to write in the names of her partners. We sat at the table with the president of the club. There were several young men and some other girls (all Dominican). The Dominican girls wore huge tulle bows in their hair, or big high combs. I wore my hair straight back and in a braid which hung below my waist. They wore rather fussy taffeta dresses, I a pale-blue voile with white organdy collar and cuffs. Whether it was because I looked so different, or what it was—anyway, I was a succès fou. The young men crowded around me signing me up and, to Father's and Mother's horror (they wanted to go home), I was booked for every dance. The dances lasted for half an hour with a fifteen-minute interval, so that the evening went on and on.

The Dominicans were wonderful dancers but there was one in particular who slithered about like a lizard in the danzón and I was carried away by the fun of it all, laughing and flirting, my braid swinging in time to my steps. This, however, was no young lieutenant in awe of the commanding officer. He pressed my hand hotly and engaged me in animated Spanish conversation as we strolled around the room between dances. My Spanish was not good enough to indulge in the sort of repartee that I felt the occasion demanded, so I asked him if he knew the words of a popular Dominican song called "Mi Amor."

"Sí, sí," he answered eagerly, then asked me to write my name and address on a piece of paper which he handed me. "Su nombre es muy dulce y muy simpático," he murmured.

Next he wanted to know my age.

"Seventeen," I said boldly, upping it by almost two and a half years.

He smiled and tucked the paper into his pocket. "Bueno," he said. "I speak English. Thank you, love."

We both laughed at that. It was all he knew but he seemed eager to learn.

A ballerina with a Pierrot

When we left, Father and Mother were very cross. "You must never do that again," said Mother. "You are too young to stay up so late. If we ever take you to another Dominican party, you must say that you can stay for only one dance. It is ridiculous, a child of your age staying up so late."

"Lots of girls at home stay up later than I do," I protested.

"And look at them," said Mother, "all worn out and wrinkled by the time they are twenty-five. Do you want to be like that?"

Twenty-five seemed so old to me that I could hardly imagine anyone's caring how she looked at that age. "Goodness, I'm all in," said Father, yawning. "Thank heaven, we will be in bed in a few minutes."

I kissed them both good night and went to my room. Frankly, I was exhausted, too, and could hardly keep my eyes open. I skimmed through my bedtime preparations, knelt and said my prayers, then climbed in under the mosquito netting and in a few minutes was sound asleep. I don't know how long I slept, but deep down in my dreams a strange tinkling noise penetrated to me and slowly pulled me up to consciousness. Half asleep, I sat up in bed. What was happening? From the garden below I could hear whispers and twangings and the scuffle of feet on the gravel path. Then, suddenly, on the air a burst of song:

> Mi amor, mi amor,
> Asómate a la ventana
> Sal y ve rosa temprana
> Que por ti estoy muriendo de amor.
>
> (My love, my love,
> Come to thy window,
> Come and see rosebud,
> For thee, I'm dying with love.)

Then, "What the hell," I heard Father shout from the next room. "Sentry!" he bellowed. "See who those people are making that noise."

"Yes, sir," stammered the sentry, who had probably been asleep.

I leapt out of bed and, rushing to the window, peered through the shutters. There were four young men, with my friend standing in the front. All of them had guitars and all were looking toward my closed windows. I should have had a rose, but there was nothing near me except a sponge on the washbasin. The thought of throwing a sponge down made me want to laugh and I did not want them to hear me laughing.

The sentry had gone into the garden but, as he could not speak a word of Spanish, nothing but excited exclamations came up to us. At this point, Mother in her dressing gown leaned out the window. "Go away," she said in Spanish. "You sing nicely but it is too late and you are waking all our neighbors. Thank you and please go home. My daughter is only thirteen and too young to be serenaded."

I felt like flinging open the shutter. What a humiliation! I would never be able to walk in the plaza again. Thirteen! What a terrible thing to say! But it did the trick. They excused themselves and Father told the sentry to return to his post. And all was quiet again.

I crept back under my mosquito netting. I only hoped that the lieutenants would not think I was thirteen.

Santiago Diary

Author's note: One thing was in my favor: my mother was a tremendous flirt. By looking through windows and stretching my neck around half-closed doors, I had learned a thing or two about flirting and decided to embark on this rather perilous course in my own life. In doing this, I felt I was approaching the grown-up world, which I somehow took to instinctively. These great passions of mine (described here) were totally a figment of my imagination. I knew nothing of the so-called facts of life and wasn't even interested. It was all a marvelous scenario about nothing!

No one but a sneak and a cad would read this diary without asking me first.

—Roberta Brooke Russell

Santo Domingo, Santiago, 1917

July 26, 1917 I have been listening to Russian music, and I want to marry a Russian peasant; a great strong beautiful brute, who would beat me, and pull me around by my hair. Yes, don't laugh. I mean it!

How I long for Morton, my heart throbs and calls for him. Great Gods how I worship him. To think of it buried alive, when the love of living is strongest.

What difference does it make? Why not eat from a trough, tie a sackcloth about you, and sleep on the ground. When one dies it is all over. You are buried. You are forgotten. Failure, success, how futile it is! I must go to sleep. The cur-rent of my thoughts is too strong. I shall go mad if I continue.

I have had my sleep, and I feel better. I have had a drive in the motor too, and the fresh air has purified my soul. I will tell you about Santiago.

It is a quaint little town with crooked streets, and low one-story houses which are painted in faded pastel shades. Sometimes one sees a two story house, but not often. There are two plazas where the band plays, and where one can walk of an evening and listen to the music.

The people are of every sort. There is the light-colored senorita, with a bow in her hair, splendid earrings in her ears, a sash about her waist, and a rose in her hand; women who ride on the horses, and donkeys, funny old women with handkerchiefs around their heads and long cigars in their mouths; withered old women with lean, brown feet; the Spanish caballero all dressed in white, who paces proudly down the street on his beast; little boys astride burroughs, small burroughs, staggering under the weight of their huge packs of Tobacco; little naked babies, perhaps adorned with a necklace of blue beads, or a pair of gold earrings, and O, hundreds of other people who I can't possibly describe. It is fascinating. . .

July 28, 1917 We had an earthquake the other night. The house rocked and creaked, but I was not afraid. I expected no good of it, if I die an obscure death, well—such is the fate of some!

August 1, 1917 All sorts of things have happened. The other day, a party of us went to old Santiago. It was destroyed by an earthquake some time ago, about a hundred years or so. The old church still remains, and, also the bath where the Spanish Knights used to bathe. It is quite a large place with steps leading down; the water comes from some unknown source. There are also the ruins of several houses. The doctor says that it was built 102 years before Jamestown. Coming home we got caught in a storm. My horse bolted and bucked, when he heard the thunder, and I was terrified; so I said to Mr. Davis "You won't leave me will you?" (O, how I wish I hadn't) and he said "Don't be afraid, of course I won't." We came home, changed our clothes, and went to a dinner at the Yaki. It was a real Dominican dinner. Everything cooked with onions. Of course I sat next to Mr. Davis. (Mr. Griffin was on the other side) How we ever found something to talk about I don't know. We have seen each other every day and every night since I have been here.

The next night we went to Mme. O'Quet's to dinner. Again champagne flowed like water, and so did every other kind of wine. Mr. Davis promised to bring me home, so we continued gaily to dance. We danced out on the porch, and he was very silent, and kept looking at me tenderly. It was all I could to do to keep from laughing. Thank heavens' for a sense of humor. It is priceless!! Imagine, he is twenty-three, and ought not to be taken in by every little chit that comes along.

Last night we went out for a drive together. It was a beautiful moonlight night and the road shone like silver. All the Dominicans ran out of their houses and looked at us, and I wondered what it was all about. Suddenly Mr. Davis began to laugh. He said "Do you know what these people think?" I looked inquiringly into his face: "No, what?"

"They think that we are engaged, because we ride in a carriage together. I wish it were so!"

I moaned "You've completely spoiled my drive."

That is a specimen of our conversation. Isn't it elevating?

August 2, 1917 We took a walk thru' the woods yesterday afternoon, Mr. Davis and I. We were very serious, at least he was. He talked about theories, and capturing of bandits, and how an officer ought to treat his men. I didn't say a word, but murmered a sympathetic "yes" now and then. He asked me if I was going to the plaza, and I said no, I was going to stay home and play solitaire. (I thought I was getting to be a regular "old woman of the sea.") Mr. Griffen came for me, and we went to the plaza and then to a party. We met Mr. Fugate, and Mr. Davis in the park. Fugy tried to be rather facetious, so I was facetious too, for I didn't want Mr. Davis to think that he was the only pebble on the beach.

At Mrs. Howlands I got a comfortable place in the swing so that I didn't want to move. I just sat there, and swung, swung into eternity. How could all of these fearful drinking people understand what I was thinking about. I thought about Morton and all the delightful things he said and did, and O, hundreds of innermost thoughts.

I danced once with Mr. Griffen, and several times with Mr. Davis. He was terribly silent, and so, I was too. He called me "dear" once, and evidently expected me to be thrilled, but I didn't turn a hair. In fact I continued talking in a matter of fact manner, and even made a feeble joke or two. Speaking of jokes, Mr. Davis said something fearfully serious, and romantic, and I don't think I took in the full significance of it, for when I began to laugh, he looked hurt, and said, "But this isn't a joking matter," whereupon I, in my cunning little facetious way, said, "My dear boy, haven't you discovered that everything is a joke with me?"

August 21, 1917 This morning I was in an awful humor when I got up, and so I prayed to the dear Lord to make me sweeter, and do you know not very long afterwards I began to think how much I adored Morton, and I tingled all over with joy. From the porch you can see the distant blue hills. They are always there but every day they are different; different lights, shadows and colors; and I thought that my love for Morton is that way, always there, and yet every day there is a new phase or feeling, and I began to think of all our glorious moments together, and I felt so happy that I had to sing.

Mr. Davis pretends to be very "épris" of me, and talks a lot about marrying and other rot. I rather encourage him, but he is depressingly "banal." I know just what he is going to say before he opens his mouth.

Mother has a vague notion about getting an English governess, and staying down here until after Christmas, but I am endeavoring to nip the thought in the bud. If there is a God in heaven, I call upon him to take pity upon a miserable sinner. Besides, I want to be useful. I want to go home and run a jitney (5 cent bus) from Quantico (officers training camp, 30 miles out of Washington, in Virginia) to Washington. I can drive a Ford now, and I think that it is a delightful scheme. Can't you see me in a fetching gray auto costume driving in a carload of dashing young officers? Oh, la, la!

The war has begun to impress me lately. It is too horrible for words. We have lost every shred of civilization, and have become nothing but fearful, blood-thirsty animals.

I would like to build me a little hut way up on a Mountain top, and live there with all my best beloved until the war is over. Everything is frenzied now, and oh, I hate to think of it.

August 22, 1917 I feel in rather a nice mood this morning, in fact I have no feeling at all. I never told you about the dance at the Eden café. Mr. Davis wrote the invitations. The Eden is awfully pretty and has a fascinating little garden and is really quite apart from the rest of the world.

They had an improvised orchestra, which was remarkably good, and which was greatly appreciated, for a victrola with antiquated records is our usual music.

Real American chicken salad and olive sandwiches were constantly served, also ice cream, cakes, punch, and any kind of drink that you wanted to order from the café. Some party, believe me! It lasted until eight o'clock in the morning, but we left at one-thirty.

Yesterday afternoon we had our usual "thé dansant" and it went off much better than usual. I took care to be nice to everyone and enjoyed myself a lot. It is very hard for me to be nice to more than one person at a time, and so I am trying to conquer that failing. Down here I have fallen into the habit of thinking that it was a bore to talk to uncongenial, unresponsive persons, but I have discovered that no matter how horrid a person may appear on the surface, if you dig deeper you will find some nice, unexpected little qualities. For instance, yesterday I was talking to young Mr. Linscott, who I had always regarded as a creature with whom soul communion was—well, out of the question. As I was saying, I was digging thru' the hard ground of uncongenial conversation with the spade of platitudes when I struck upon a gold mine. I could have screamed with joy. He likes to read!! His eyes are bad, and my eyes are bad, so he is coming here twice a week and we are going to read aloud, taking turns. C'est entendu! Twice a week!

I think that "Bon Dieu" must have heard me praying yesterday morning.

I am going riding with Dr. Drefus, and Mr. Davis this afternoon at half-past four. Dr. Drefus is very good-looking and clever (so Mother tells me). I heard him talking about Darwin's "Origin of Species," so I fancy he delves in rather far.

My horse's name is "Musty," Father's is "Dick," Mother's is "Hungry." I write all this down, so if I ever read this at a future time, I will remember my rides at Santiago.

The rides around here are very pretty. I try to take a lot of exercise for I am supposed to be very anemic. I never heard such rot, if you could see me, I am as strong as a horse.

Mother hasn't ridden since her fall and is afraid for me too, but I shan't stop. No, not I.

Some one told me last night that the first casualty list would come home on the 27th. Isn't that terrible. Won't it be horrible at home, where the fathers and brothers and sons begin to go. O, why was I ever born into this dreadful time! Why couldn't my soul have waited a little longer!

August 23, 1917 I had the most wonderful ride yesterday. We started out on the old Santiago road, and then branched off into a little footpath. The green boughs of the trees met over our heads, and there was a carpet of soft grass beneath our horses feet.

Mr. Davis and I had a race, but poor old "Musty" is not very speedy, so I must admit that I was worsted. The dinner at the officers' mess went off splendidly, and I was enchanted with everything. After dinner we took a little walk in the park, and for about five minutes Mr. Davis and I were alone. He said, "Brooke, do you know that you are the sweetest thing in all the world," whereupon I, having been told that before by various ardent suitors, laughed sceptically, and softly, and looked the other way. Is there nothing new in the world? Can one find a phrase, a look, a gesture that is not hackneyed.

Dare I admit that after this tirade that I rather

thrilled at these words, I don't remember, but I am afraid I did. Well anyway, we were just putting on our bathing suits preparatory to the plunge into the deep sea of intense conversation, when along came Mother, with three young officers, and sat down beside us.

It seems that Mr. Griffen, and Mr. Fugate went and told Mother that, "that fellow Davis never gives us a chance to talk to Miss Brooke," so she decided to come and break us up.

For an hour I sat on the bench between Mr. Fugate and Mr. Griffen and carried on a conversation, which means that I shook the leaves from every tree of knowledge.

August 24, 1917 We went up to parade yesterday afternoon, and took little Albert. Albert is too cute for words, and when I hold him it is all I can do to keep from squeezing him to death. I wouldn't own this to any but you, for I pretend to abhor children, and I do if I hear a lot of women sitting around talking about them in a stupid, disgusting way, and if I have to take care of them, but otherwise they are not bad.

Mr. Davis was on duty, so he wasn't there. Yes, I missed him awfully, and was rather bored without him.

Mr. Griffen made love to me, but I was too weary to turn an eyelash. He told me heart rending stories of cruel desertions which he had experienced, and that he had done with all women except me, that he adored me, and always would—in fact he got off the usual line in the usual manner; and if I closed my eyes I would have thought I was home listening to

Charlie, or Bobby, or Chippy. Am I to be eternally bored by that sort of rot. I think they think that that is what girls like but if they would only realize how hackneyed it is!

August 25, 1917 I am going home a month from to-day. Do you hear—going home! What ecstasy! What a happy lot mine will be then!

August 26, 1917 Yesterday I had a wonderful ride. Mr. Davis and I raced together and a bull chased us, and Heaven' knows what else.

Mr. Davis says that a good rider must appear to the world as if he didn't care a darn what his horse did, and yet really to care a lot. I get frightened now and then, but I want to please Mr. Davis, so I pretend to be very happy-go-lucky. It is rather hard to laugh and joke when your horse is rearing at a palm leaf, or racing down a steep, sandy, slidy hill, but I try awfully hard. I realize now that all that he used to tell me in the beginning about liking timid girls was nothing but hot air. Ah, the gay deceiver! Man is a protean they say, and I don't know.

Mother is reading Henry Esmond aloud to me now, and altho' I have read it before I adore it. There is no one like Thackeray in my opinion.

On glancing over this diary I find not a single word about reading. I love to read better than anything else, but my eyes have been so bad that writing in this diary is the only time I use them during the day. I am not such a vapid creature as this book makes me appear. I don't know, perhaps I am. How can I tell?

August 27, 1917 The Bentons had a delicious dinner, out on their "patio." Their patio overlooks the river, and the moon on the water was too lovely for words.

After dinner we went inside, and Mrs. Benton played the piano, and she and I sang together.

Finally realizing that Mr. Davis was getting silent, all alone in his corner, she asked me to take him out, and show him the moon. So I did, and we stayed there all evening.

We sat in the hammock, and wanted to turn light off, only were afraid that Mrs. Benton might not think it nice.

I don't know whether I looked nice or not. I had on a white dress, and a white sash, with a red rose on my belt. Very fetching, you say, well, rather!

I told Mr. Davis that I thought he was a gay deceiver, and told him why; whereupon the dear lad blushed and said that I didn't understand him. It seems that he likes very feminine young ladies, or the clinging vine type (he didn't say so, but so I imagine from his remarks) who are sweet and fluffy and yet with all that look well on a horse, and can do everything with poise (his words). I said "very good, Eddie* (his name is Edward), and laughed skeptically.

We carried on an animated discussion. I said that men never have very strong passions, that they could never love as women could (dangerous groun? Yes, but that's the sport.) He replied, "You read that in novels, and all novelists are

*Very Good Eddie is the name of a popular musical comedy.

liars. Why, every man is a sentamentalist down in his heart, and imagines himself fighting his way to some fair lady, who will drop him a rose." Me shrugging my shoulders—"A sentamentalist, yes, but where is the man who has real feeling.

They love sometimes of course, but only as a child loves a toy, or a dog, or something. Don't tell me! I know what I am talking about."

At this time we got so interested in looking at each other, that we sort of lost the thread, and began another topic.

My eyes hurt I must stop.

August 28, 1917 Yesterday afternoon we went up to the canteen. Well, anyway we went up there and found young Mr. Miller, who has just come up from Monte Christe. He is very good-looking, but is not quite such a "spiritual" type as Mr. Davis.

I was so elated at finding new prey, that a little later when I was driving the car I went into a ditch. Father and Mother were saying their prayers in the back seat, and it was only because Metty [the chauffeur] put on the brake, that we weren't all killed. You see I had on the reverse and was trying to turn!! I never thought of looking behind me, or of going slowly. It was really rather funny!

August 29, 1917 Mr. Davis is rather pathetic. When he called me up he told me he had been trying to have a hammock made to surprise me, but he hadn't been able to get it. When I thought of the poor thing slaving away to please me I almost wept. Men are really terribly pathetic, and I think that if Mr. Davis were new, there would be no comparison between him and Mr. Miller. As it is, I like them both about the same.

August 30, 1917 I went out riding with Mr. Davis yesterday afternoon, and he came here to see me last night. We talked about the difference between customs in Richmond and Washington. Down south a girl can go anywhere alone with a man, while in the north, one has to be strictly chaperoned. He took my hand early in the evening, but I took it quickly away and said, "No, please. Ours is a very platonic relationship." Later, he made another attempt, and when he said "Do you mind very much," I said "I don't know, I was just trying to decide whether I do or not," whereupon we both laughed and the strain was relieved.

Morton was better at that sort of thing than anyone I have ever met. He used to get me worked up to such a state that I was just asking to—O, suppose someone should read this!

I sometimes think that I am falling in love with him, but no, of course not. I wonder whether I would think he was nice if I saw him at home, and I wonder if he looks nice in "cits" (civilian clothes). I imagine he wears a gold watch chain draped across his front, and a soft green felt hat! Ugh! I'm afraid he does.

September 3, 1917 I am weary of Life. I am only happy about half an hour a day, and sometimes not that much. O, ye gods! Why was I born. I am stupid, and never will be any good to anyone.

September 14, 1917 Every now and then I get these fits, and then I wonder if there is such a thing as a tranquil life. To all appearances in my life, to-day is like yesterday and to-morrow will be like to-day, but Dios, how my feelings change. I may be happy to-morrow!

Last night Mother and Father took a walk and so I was alone. I sat in the hammock and looked at the stars, and ate caramels. The Cape-lo's played sympathetic music on the pianola and I felt radiantly happy. Whenever I look up at the sky when I am all alone I fairly tingle with happiness.

It is wonderful. I feel as tho' rays of light must be coming from my face.

I am sorry I am growing-up. When I was small, life was so mysterious. I felt convinced that I was a kidnapped princess, and that some day my father and mother, the king and queen would find me, then I would go live in a palace, and wear beautiful clothes and jewels, and have one hundred adoring princes at my feet. I was also convinced that I was going to be a beauty, and now when I know I am not—well it is depressing to be ugly, say what you will. Every-time I look at myself in the glass I feel sick.

September 17, 1917 When I woke up this morning I wanted to go to sleep again for I thought "O what is the use of waking up." Just then Mother came in and said "Would you like to go to Moca?" O heavens, how pleased I was. I jumped up and got dressed, and we started. Mother and Major Miller and I in one car and Father, Colonel Marix and an orderlie in another.

It was a divine ride. We bumped and rattled, and got stuck in the mud, and got out and walked, and crossed rivers, and everything else. The country was lovely, we drove through cacao plantations, banana plantations, palm tree groves, little villages, with squatty houses, great meadows, wild green jungle, and everything else.

We took luncheon with Captain Miller at "Moca." He is charming, an Annapolis graduate with a great deal of "savoir faire."

I was a bit surprised at having our cock-tails in a bedroom but I soon got over it.

Mr. Davis and I went to the park last night. He said that he couldn't keep his vow. Well! He got sentimental, but after egging him on to that state I didn't want him that way. When he would say something particularly adoring, I would pretend I didn't notice it, and continue talking.

O, ye gods, what a life. I love to have them adoring, but not jealous, or humble. A little jealousy is all right, but this doubting everyone—no!

Mr. Davis is more than I can handle. He is as serious as Solomon, only more so. He—O, I can't explain. Suppose some sneaking cad were to read this book!

October 11, 1917 Weeks have passed like days, hours like minutes since I last wrote. We have been having picnics, donkey-rides, dances, and etc. Life is gay here.

Mr. Davis has been behaving foolishly, extremely foolishly. He took me out driving in a cache one night and when I told the man to turn and go back, he said he would shoot him if he did. So there we stood. I was terrified. He wanted to kiss me, and told me that he was alone. But finally I persuaded him to turn back, without any effects.

October 16, 1917 On the boat bound for home! I feel sad, sadder than I like to admit, sadder than the sad sea waves.

Everything is behind me, the picnics, the donkey-rides, the "cache" rides, the violent love-making,—and Father!!! What is Mr. Davis doing I wonder?

There is a revolution in Haiti, and father has gone over. Poor, patient, just adorable Father.

The night before we left Santiago they had a party. Everybody came to say good-bye to us. Mr. Davis played poker but took me home.

October 17, 1917 Still at sea. Ye gods, how she rolls! How bored I am. Soon we will be home.

Morton will not be there. How sad! Who will it be this winter? It must be someone I can not live without intense moments! One when he leans forward almost touched you and you know that he would give everything he owns to just kiss you once! Yes, it is nice and I take it as my due.

I like it; it is meat and drink.

Poor Father all alone. I hate to think of it.

I can't think. I shall stop.

Chapter 16

Incarceration

When we returned from Santo Domingo, Mother had decided that she would put me into boarding school until Easter and go back to spend the time with Father in Santiago. This project was a tremendous surprise, as I had been told nothing of it, and I wept bitterly when the subject was first broached. I had never been without my family and I hated the whole idea. Mother was adamant, though, and she sallied forth to Miss Madeira's to tell Miss Madeira that I was to be a boarder. However, Miss Madeira was not at the school, and a younger mistress said, yes, they could squeeze me in as a boarder as I was an old day pupil, but when she started in on the curriculum, Mother blew up.

"Imagine," she said later to Granny, "this ridiculous young teacher insisted that they could not enroll Brooke again unless she took a lot of, to my mind, perfectly absurd subjects, so that she could pass a college-board examination."

"College," said Granny. "Goodness me, what does Brooke want to go to college for?"

"Well, that's just it, Mama [pronounced ma*ma*]," said Mother. "Naturally I don't want Brooke to go to college. Madeira's has really become very highhanded. I was absolutely furious, so what do you suppose I did?"

"What?" said Granny.

"What?" I echoed.

"Well," said Mother triumphantly, "I took a cab right up to Holton-Arms and had a most delightful talk with Mrs. Holton, and she is going to take Brooke there."

"Oh, no!" I cried. "Why did you do that?"

Mother looked at me and smiled. "Because I am not going to be bullied by some whippersnapper of a schoolmistress. We discussed what subjects Brooke should take and decided on English literature and history, history of art, French, Latin, and music; not any more, as Brooke's eyes aren't strong."

"Law," said Granny, "it seems quite a lot to me."

"I don't want to go to Holton," I said. "I want to go back to Madeira. All my best friends are there, and just because I pass a college-board exam doesn't mean that I *have* to go to college."

"You know lots of girls at Holton," said Mother. "Evie and Nancy and Katie and Alice, I can't remember them all, just as many as you know at Madeira. Anyway, it is only until Easter, and I saw the rooms at Holton and they are very attractive."

"What's going to happen to our house?" I asked. "Is it going to be all shut up?" "No," said Mother. "I've let it to Mazarin from the Banque Franco-Chinois. He loves it and will take good care of it."

I was stunned by Mother's efficiency and must have looked bewildered. Granny took my hand. "Precious," she said, "your old granny will be right here and you can come and see her whenever you feel like it."

I was unable to speak, so shook my head violently. I was more knowledgeable than Granny and I knew that boarders were far from free and could go out only so many times a month. The whole thing seemed a nightmare, and I prayed with all my heart and soul that it would never be realized. The die was cast, though, and when the day finally arrived I clung desperately to Mother in the drawing room of the school. Mother was weeping violently, too.

"I hate to leave you, darling," she kept saying, and added, "but Father has been alone so much and you will find it fun being with girls your own age all the time."

I knew that I would hate girls if I had to be with them all the time, but I gulped back my protests. Mother tore herself away at last and I stood in the doorway waving as she disappeared down S Street, fluttering her handkerchief from the window of the cab. The taxi turned into Connecticut Avenue and I turned back into the hall and went gloomily to my room. Another girl was already there busily hanging up banners and putting photographs around.

"My name is Audrey G.," she said, "and my father is a famous painter and the reason I am at school is because he has just married for the fourth time and doesn't want me around." She

An illustration I copied from Vogue

seemed quite pleased about it and looked at me as though to challenge me to relate anything as interesting as that. I thought it rather horrible and knew that I would be ashamed of Father if *he* had married four times. "I am going to be an actress," she continued. "My father says that all women need an emotional outlet apart from men. A woman who depends entirely on a man for all her emotional life is lost." She laughed. "*He* should know. Women are mad about him. He's terribly attractive."

I sat down on my bed. What a funny girl. How could she talk about her family like that? She was pretty, with curly black hair and cream-colored skin, and I knew that she was being friendly. *I* was the one, as usual, who seemed to have nothing to say.

"What's your name?" she asked.

"Brooke Russell," I answered, "and I want to be a poetess, or perhaps a nun." I folded my hands in my lap and tried to look like a nun, saintly and removed from the world.

"Are you a Catholic?" she asked.

"No," I answered.

"Then you can't become a nun," she said triumphantly and continued fixing up her corner of the room.

We spent six weeks in that room together, then we had to be separated, as we fought like cat and dog. We were really too much alike. *I* wanted to be an actress, but she had said it first, and that rankled, as playing the nun wasn't nearly so much fun. As far as temperament and fire were concerned, I would not concede to anyone. I liked her in spite of our fights because I understood her, and she liked me, but we waged a constant war of survival.

The whole situation was brought to a head by an absurd incident. In the graduating class, and therefore older than we, was a very attractive Canadian girl. Audrey and I both admired her enormously. We had what was then called a "crush" on her, and followed her around, imitating her voice and gestures and walk. We worshiped everything about her, and when one day we heard that she was going to have a sale of clothes in her room, we of course went to get a souvenir of the "loved one." Upon arrival, we spotted at the same moment a delicious brown beaver hat, with a high crown and a brown ribbon cockade on the side.

"Oh, how divine," we cried simultaneously. It seemed almost too good to be true that it not only belonged to the loved one but was also chic and suitable.

"I saw it first," said Audrey.

"No, I did," I said. "Look, I'm holding it."

"Only because I took my hand away," retorted Audrey. "Don't be a swine. You know I saw it first."

"You are a liar and you know you are," I said, and pushed away her predatory hand.

Edith, who was the subject of our admiration and the owner of the hat, came over. "What on earth are you two fighting about?"

"The hat," I said, and not wanting to appear too awful before this divine creature, I added that we had both seen it at the same time and both wanted it.

Edith laughed. "Why, that's easy," she said. "You are roommates, so why don't you buy it together, and one wear it one day and the other wear it the next?"

Audrey gave a cry of joy. "Oh, Edith," she said, "how marvelous you are, and how stupid we were not to have thought of it." She gave me a bright smile.

I smiled, too. "Thank you, dear Edith," I murmured, but as I paid the $2.50 that was my share I had misgivings. We bore the hat back to our room and tried it on. It looked better on Audrey, but I stuffed my braid up under the crown and pinned a long brown veil to the brim. Even Audrey grudgingly admitted that I looked very sophisticated.

"Mrs. Holton will never let you go out on the street like that," she said smugly. (Mrs. Holton always examined us with a sharp eye on the days we went visiting.)

"She won't see me," I retorted. "I will pin it on in the drugstore."

At the end of their magnificent dance, a floored audience

Alas, the next day I got a bad case of pink eye and went to the infirmary. During my enforced stay there I heard that Audrey was out every day in "our" hat, and as I told one and all around me, I was "absolutely livid." "Wait until I get out," I said threateningly.

"Why do you care?" said the girl in the next bed. "You can't wear it when you're sick."

That was perfectly logical, but the idea that I had paid my share and was getting no use out of it infuriated me. "She is probably getting it all filthy," I said, "and it will be a putrid mess when I want to wear it." (It was the fashion at school to be rather overemphatic in one's speech.)

At last the day came when my eyes cleared and I returned to my room. I had arranged to go to tea that afternoon with Monsieur Mazarin at our house, and I knew that Monsieur Casenave was to be there. I wanted to look my best. I did not think that I dared wear the veil, as I knew Monsieur Casenave would write Mother, but I *did* want to wear *my new hat.*

As I entered the room there was Audrey combing her hair, looking very smart in a red dress, and on her bed—the hat. "Oh, hello," she said. "You are little Bright Eyes again."

"Yes," I said, "and I am going out to tea with some friends of Mother's."

"I'm going out, too," she said. "Daddy and his wife are taking me to the Spanish embassy. Daddy's new wife comes from an old Spanish family, you know."

"Really," I said. "What fun for you," and I looked at the hat. Audrey followed my eyes.

"You don't mind if I wear it today?" she said. "It looks rather Spanish when I tilt it on the side. Look," she picked it up and put it on at a rakish angle over her dark curls.

"Would you mind awfully if I wore it today?" I asked. "Your red velvet tam looks very pretty with that dress."

"Oh, I *hate* that tam," cried Audrey. "This hat is much nicer." She looked at herself in her hand mirror.

"I'd like to wear it," I said, falsely quiet. "I haven't seen Mother's friends all winter, and I do want to look nice."

"Why don't you wear your blue hat with the beaver fur bow," she said, "the one that matches your coat?" I knew it matched the coat and I supposed it was more suitable but I was determined to wear "our" hat.

"You've been wearing the hat every day," I said, trying to be calm, "and I think you are being piggish in not letting me have it the day I come out of the infirmary. After all, it's just as much *my* hat as it is yours."

Audrey, who still had the hat on her head, stamped her foot. "That has nothing to do with it," she snapped. "I told you that this was a very special occasion, much more important than an ordinary tea, and you are the piggish one to want to spoil everything for me. Anyway, you can't have it. *I* am going to keep it right on my head until I go out."

At that I saw red. "You *are* not!" I cried, jumping up and snatching it off her head. She tried to yank it out of my hand, but I held fast. We tugged and pulled, our faces red and our breath coming in gasps. Finally I gave a tremendous tug, and was horrified to find myself falling to the floor. The wretched hat had been torn apart and I lay on the floor with the brim in my hand while Audrey had the crown. It was indeed the decision of a Solomon! We both burst into tears and continued sobbing insults.

All this had not been exactly quiet, and must have been heard through the entire floor. Miss Ingalls, the mistress in charge, opened our door and looked in at us in consternation. "What is this awful row?" We both tried to explain at once, naturally presenting the case to our own advantage. Miss Ingalls would, however, have none of it. "You are two stupid little girls," she said. "You should know better. You each get five demerits, and *neither* of you can go out to tea. You have to learn how to behave. You are acting like babies." We pleaded against this harsh verdict, but she was adamant and left us to bitter recriminations and the giggles and mock sympathy of the other girls on the floor.

The upshot of this incident was that I was moved to a room of my own. It was one of the few single rooms, and was tiny, but I could close my door and give myself up to daydreaming without interference.

It was really very hard to live in the city that was my home and yet not *be* at home. For the girls from other parts of the country it was an experience just to be in Washington. The school itself was lodged in adjoining houses, all very gay and homelike, and the teachers from Mrs. Holton down were sympathetic and intelligent. But I hated every minute of it. For me those few months had a slightly nightmarish quality. The familiar streets seemed strange when I walked with a group of girls, shepherded by the teachers. Dear Dupont Circle made me feel like crying just to walk through it, and at the corner of De Sales Street and Connecticut Avenue I could hardly bear to look down the street toward our house or even to see the bare branches of the trees rising over the convent wall.

I lunched with Granny and Grandfather every other Sunday, but I cried so hard when I had to leave that it was not a pleasure for any of us.

The worst of all was having tea at our house with Monsieur Mazarin, who had rented it. I only went once, as it was too upsetting an experience to be repeated. Monsieur Mazarin may have loved the house, but his was a form of love that took everything and gave nothing in return. The poor house looked ashamed of itself—rundown, dirty, and utterly neglected. Even the little gate had come off its hinge so that it swung disconsolately, unable to do its job of keeping out intruders. Mazarin had brought some flowers and had stuck them stiffly in a vase, but this gesture was like a bit of jewelry on a disheveled person. There were alcohol rings on the tables, the chintz looked dirty, there was dust everywhere, the lampshades and window shades were crooked, and the windowpanes dirty. It was all I could do

Types of Greenwich Village

The Vorticist.

The superbly-indifferent Poetess.

The young society Woman.

The demure school girl.

The vivacious adventuress

The emancipated old maid.

The poor young artist

The artists model.

to keep from bursting into tears. Monsieur Casenave and Monsieur Tardieu also were there, so I had to make conversation, and I tried to be funny about school. I even told the story of the hat, which made them laugh inordinately. "Comme elles sont drôles, les jeunes filles américaines," roared Mazarin. He asked me to pour the tea when his Tonkinese servant brought in the tea tray, and I did so in my most jeune-fille-turning-woman-of-the-world manner but my heart was not in it when I saw the blackness of the silver (Mother had left everything for Mazarin) and the chipped teacups.

When it was time to leave I wondered if I ever could bear to see the house again, or if even Mother could bring it to life. Monsieur Casenave took me back to school in his car, and when we were alone he took my hand. "Don't be so sad, Brooke," he said. "I know you miss your mother terribly, but she will be back soon. Just think of that. School cannot be so very bad."

At this encouragement, although he had never been a confidant of mine, the floodgates were opened and I poured out my heart to him. I was very, very homesick and I hated being bottled up with a lot of girls. I said that they were so messy and insensitive and boring.

Monsieur Casenave had hardly a chance to speak, but as we drove up to the door he gave me a bit of advice. "Try to meditate a little each day," he said, "in your room, in the morning or in the evening. Try to think of something beautiful, a bit of prose, or a picture, or a landscape. Put all thoughts of yourself away and concentrate on a bit of beauty. I know that it will help you."

I *did* try, and it did help, and I liked Monsieur Casenave much better than I ever had.

At last the Easter holidays came around and it was time for Mother's return. I was wild with joy, and when I drove up to Granny's house (we were to stay there a few days while our house was being cleaned) and found Granny, and Grandfather, and Mother all there, I danced the Highland fling in the Green

Room and out through the hall and around the dining-room table.

So ended my career at boarding school. The only thing I learned from constant association with girls my age was that after you have washed a handkerchief, if you stick it on the mirror to dry, it will come out almost as if it were ironed!

"Monsieur Casenave was very nice to me," I said to Mother later that day and told her what he had said.

"He is very wise," answered Mother. "I am glad that you have learned to appreciate him."

"But he looks like a monkey," I said.

Mother laughed. "Yes, that's part of his charm. At least that's what your father and I think, and sometimes he looks like Master François Rabelais, laughing in his easy chair."

I laughed. How delicious it was to be really at home again!

In concluding this chapter I might add that I went to the two best schools in Washington and was taught by competent teachers, but my interest in Grown-up conversation at home was so strong that at school I simply rejected everything that would not help me hold my own in the drawing room.

Today I can recite almost all *The Canterbury Tales* in Middle English. I can quote from *Le Rouge et le Noir*, the characters in Dickens and Thackeray and Fielding are my friends, but I can hardly add a column of figures and any scientific fact goes in one ear and out the other. So what knowledge I have is a hodge-podge. At least I am fully aware of this and, in the subjects that interest me, continue to have fun educating myself.

Chapter 17

The Prom

When the telephone bell rang I was sitting at the table in the window of our upstairs sitting room in Washington. I was busily painting a model I had copied from *Vogue*. I was painting her large straw hat yellow, and the roses on the crown pale and deep pink. It was an absorbing task, and it was only when I heard Mother mention my name that I stopped to lick my paintbrush and listen. "Oh, I don't really think I could let Brooke do that," Mother was saying. "She's really too young." The person on the other end of the line continued talking and Mother's face grew thoughtful. "Yes, I *do* see," she said, "and, of course, *you* would be there. I tell you what. May I think it over until this evening and call you back?" The person talked a bit more and Mother smiled. "Well, it's nice of you to say that." She looked across at me. "I will call you tonight," and she hung up.

"What is it?" I asked excitedly.

"Mrs. T.," said Mother, picking up Walt Whitman's *Leaves of Grass*. "Joan has the measles and can't go to the Princeton prom with her brother, and Mrs. T. wants you to fill in."

I was struck dumb. What a thought! Joan was one of my best friends (a member of the Facio Club) but her brother I hardly knew at all. He was four years older and had once or twice called us down when we were convulsed with giggles or talked for an hour on the telephone when he wanted to use it himself. I stood in awe of him, and was fascinated that he should want me to go to the prom. Had he been secretly in love with me all this time? It was a glorious thought.

Mother seemed to sense my thought process. "He is desperate," she said. "It is too late now for him to get an attractive girl, and so Mrs. T. suggested you. He has all his dance cards filled, and rooms booked, and she thought it a pity that he had no one."

I felt indignant and humiliated. After all, the lieutenants in Santo Domingo had found me attractive, and I was almost sixteen. Who was he, at twenty, to snoot down on me? Did he read Walt Whitman and the de Goncourts? Had he ever kissed a girl

(previous page)
I seem to be advancing.
Drawn at age fifteen.

in the Caribbean moonlight? I returned to my painting and was adding bright green leaves to the roses on the hat when the telephone rang again.

It was my youngest aunt (Tantee, as I called her) and my favorite. She had come to live in Washington because her husband was in the Naval Reserve on duty at the Navy Department. Mother talked to her about this and that. (Mother looked down on her sisters as not being intellectuals; their conversation bored her.) The conversation lagged and, for want of something to say, Mother told Tantee of my invitation. "Ridiculous, of course," added Mother. "She is much too young."

"Not at all." I heard Tantee's voice ringing loud and clear. "For heaven's sake, Mabel, she is almost sixteen, and will be beautifully chaperoned. Mrs. T. is the most conservative woman in the world. Why not let her go? She might never be asked again, and something like this is such fun for a girl."

"I refuse to have her turn into a flapper," snapped Mother. "I can't bear these odious American girls whose families seem to have no control over them. I have sacrificed myself over and over again in order to see that Brooke should appreciate the amenities of life and have proper standards and be well brought up. So I refuse to have her head turned and all my teachings and sacrifices go for nothing."

Tantee lowered her voice so that I could not hear her, but whatever she said aggravated Mother and she slammed down the receiver. She lit a cigarette and picked up her Walt Whitman. And I added a blue sash to the model I was painting. (I was engaged in doing a page of fashions for the *Facio Magazine*—one copy a month—and I had a deadline to meet.) My mind, however, was not really on my work. I imagined myself, like Zuleika Dobson, taking Princeton by storm. Was there water nearby so that the whole student body could drown themselves for love of me? Would I be demure or flirtatious? Could I perhaps dress all in black, as though mourning a lover? Could I saunter under the leafy shade (I supposed they had trees

The Mocking Bird

(left and right)
A few dress designs

there), twirling a frilly parasol over my shoulder, a little Pomeranian frisking at my feet, like Chekhov's *Lady with a Dog*? "Oh, no." I could hear myself laughing. "You really mustn't talk like that. You are just being a foolish boy. I want to live before I settle down. One must learn before one loves." I would be the toast of the place, dazzling all by my beauty and my wit. I would scatter my favors impartially—one could kiss my hand, another my forehead or my hair. Another would be astonished by the depth and inscrutability of my nature. I would be a smiling enigma—gay, serious, intellectual, intangible.

There were several reasons, though, why this picture could never become true and, tearing the veil from my fantasy, I had to face the facts: (a) Joan's brother, Jack, did not really like me; (b) I was certainly far from beautiful; (c) I was habitually tongue-tied before strangers. These were all impediments to a sensational triumph, and I began to think that I had better not go at all. I would surely end up weeping in the coatroom, a wretched failure, and a complete discredit to Jack.

Mother was deep in her huge illustrated volume of Walt Whitman, and I knew that I should not interrupt but felt impelled to speak.

"I don't think I really want to go," I said softly.

"What?" said Mother, looking up from her book and keeping her finger on her place. "What are you saying?"

"I'm saying that I don't think I really want to go," I repeated. "I wouldn't know anybody, and I'm sure that I would look awful."

"You don't have to know anyone," said Mother. "Jack has everything all arranged, and Mrs. T. would be with you all the time, and as for looking awful, what do you mean? You dress as well as any other girl."

"Well, I just know I would look awful," I said. "I'm too fat and my hair is still in a braid. I'd look a mess!"

"Oh, you would have to put your hair up," said Mother, taking her hand from her place in the book. "You would have to wear it either in a braid on top of your head, or in a bun at the back."

The telephone rang again, and this time she went into her own room to answer it, closing the door behind her. I continued dreamily to paint the blue sash, to the accompaniment of her low voice. When she returned it was to tell me that all was settled. Granny had called urging Mother to let me go, and had finally overruled all objections. Mother had then called Mrs. T., who was delighted and said she was positive that as Jack could not have his sister he would be happy to have me.

I knew differently. Jack had really wanted to take a girl he was keen on, but his mother had begged him to take his little sister; he was a very good young man, devoted to his family, and so had given in. I, of course, was "any port in a storm," and the consciousness that I was a poor second choice shook my self-confidence. Because it was supposed to be great fun to go to a prom, I boasted about it at school and at the Facio Club meetings, but in my heart I knew there was nothing to be proud of, no one really wanted me. Jack was not waiting for me mad with impatience, and I received no letters or telegrams such as girls did in novels.

As we had only a week in which to get ready for the great event, all was bustle and activity. The reliable Stella was called on, and some dresses were hastily put together. Tantee had a white chiffon which had shrunk in being cleaned, and she could no longer get into it. The dress was brought over to our house, and I put it on under the speculative eyes of Granny, Mother, Tantee, and Stella. I thought it beautiful. It had panels of cobwebby silver lace floating on the skirt, and silver lace in the front of the décolleté. Little puffed sleeves of white chiffon were added and the décolleté was lifted up with white tulle. Granny bought some silver slippers for me and Grandfather contributed silk stockings with clocks up the sides. I gave a dress rehearsal when all was finished, and everyone conceded that I looked remarkably well. My hair, very heavy and long and slippery, was difficult to keep up. Mother and Tantee tried to fluff it out at the sides, but in two minutes it was as flat as a pancake, so they gave up, and I ended looking like a drowned rat. I decided to wear it skinned back from my face, wrapped in a coiled bun at the back. In order to keep it in place I had to use huge long tortoiseshell hairpins, which seemed to bore right through my head and gave me a headache. I wanted to wear spats as a final touch of sophistication, but the family drew the line there.

When all was in readiness I looked just what I was, a rather dumpy little schoolgirl. I had no aids to make me more attractive, no permanent wave, no lipstick, no rouge, and the only powder, something called papier poudré, came in a tiny book that fitted in one's purse; one pulled out a leaf and rubbed it on the nose to take the shine off. Thus equipped, I went forth with Mrs. T. to face the world, knowing that I would have to compete with "fast" girls in low-necked dresses who danced cheek to cheek, their fannies sticking out provocatively. These girls had at their command an everlasting flow of snappy talk, and a great many of them would think nothing of going out to "neck" in a car and taking a swig of hootch from a flask. By training, and by instinct, these things were alien to me. I felt that the wrath of God would descend on me if I disobeyed the teachings of my family. However, I had a deep-rooted desire to attract, and I was bursting with good health and enthusiasm.

Jack met us at Princeton Junction with a taxi. As we got into it a red Stutz Bearcat roared by us with its cutout open. I caught a glimpse of a blue-eyed young man at the wheel, and a girl smoking a cigarette beside him. I must have looked interested because Jack said, "That's the manager of the *Daily Princetonian*. You have a dance with him tonight." My heart sank. It was fun to look at people like that, but I did not feel prepared to meet them, particularly as the girl had deep crimson lips and spit curls on her cheeks. How could I ever hold the attention of a man used to such sophistication?

We spent the day mostly at the Ivy Club, sitting around the

piano, singing and talking. Mrs. T. stuck close to me, and I was grateful, although without her I knew that I could have done a rendition of "O Johnny, O Johnny, How You Can Love" or "The Dark Town Strutters' Ball" that would have really wowed them. Mrs. T. was very sedate indeed, certainly more prim than Mother, and I did not want to get in her bad graces. Actually, she did me a very good turn, because by evening I was longing to be on my own and really have a chance to show off a bit. As she helped me with my white evening dress, she said, "You look sweet, Brooke," but even in the little boarding-house bedroom where we were staying, I did not look like a future belle of the ball. The dress that had looked so pretty at home looked very childish to me, with the puffed sleeves and filled-in neck. The only way to make it come to life was to dance actively, so that the silver lace panels would float out around me. I bit my lips and pinched my cheeks to make them rosy, and followed Mrs. T. feeling like a lamb being led to slaughter. There was an attractive buffet dinner first at a private house, and Jack was wonderful. He stayed by my side, and when I seemed unable to talk to anyone else, we talked of his sister Joan, and Miss Madeira's School, and what a shame it was that Joan could not be there, which of course brought us back to the fact that if she had been there *I* would not have been. We skirted around that, and Jack brought some more people to meet me and then it was time to go to the prom.

When Mrs. T. and I went into the ladies' cloakroom, it was already crowded. I had never seen so many dazzling girls before in my life. They looked really more like Grown-ups than girls, but I supposed that quite a few of them were already "out" and so could be counted as officially Grown-up. They all had real evening dresses, slinky chiffons and satins, and tulle around their necks, and lipstick, and feather fans, and a great many had bobbed hair held in place with barrettes at the side. They sprayed themselves with perfume, and shouted to one another. New York and Philadelphia girls, I supposed, as I had never seen any of them before. I looked at myself in the glass. What a wretched homemade creature I was, no dash or chic. My heart sank to my boots.

"How do I look?" I asked Mrs. T. gravely.

She smiled benignly. "You look sweet," she said.

Sweet! Who wanted to talk to a sweet girl? A sort of gawky female Penrod.

I followed her dejectedly into the huge gymnasium, where Meyer Davis and his band were already in full swing. Jack danced the first dance with me, and pointed out some of the "men" I was going to dance with. I kept turning my head to look at them, and in doing so was constantly out of step. I realized that anyone watching me would think me a pill. A silly-looking baby and a bad dancer. However, as the evening wore on, I began to enjoy it. I knew the words of all the tunes, and if I ran out of conversation I began to sing. That made me dance better, too, as I could concentrate more on my partner.

Suddenly, at the end of a dance, Jack brought up Mr. L., the manager of the *Daily Princetonian,* and I found myself looking into the blue eyes of the young man I had seen at the station that morning. He was one of those people who just shuffle about, but he compensated for it by holding me at a distance so that we could see each other's faces.

"I saw you this morning at the station," he said, "and I have been thinking of you ever since. You have such amusing eyes."

I lost my step here, but it did not matter, he was such a poor dancer. We moved slowly about the floor, to the strains of "Poor Butterfly," a menace to all the good dancers, but I did not care anymore because his conversation was fascinating.

He guided me off the dance floor to a sofa. "Let's sit this one out and talk," he said.

What a relief! I bit my lips to make them red, and smiled at him. "Tell me about yourself," I said. "It's such fun to meet a new person. Tell me what you like to do, and what you are like." (I was cribbing a bit from some things I had heard Mother say.)

It worked. He started off and I was entranced. He was president of one of the Princeton Debating Societies. He was president of the New Jersey Audubon Society (he explained some of the delights of bird-watching), and—to him most important of all—he was one of the seven Neorealists of the world. Professor Spaulding was the founder of this philosophy. I looked on my new friend with awe. That he should be intelligent enough to be one of seven! "'We are seven,' " I murmured.

"What are you saying?" he asked laughingly.

"Wordsworth," I answered, then off he started quoting poetry, rather dull poetry by Wordsworth and Tennyson and Longfellow, but still he seemed to have a marvelous memory. He explained to me that he had never gone to school, but had been educated entirely by tutors. He seemed almost another patchwork, like myself. I found him so sympathique that I was rather annoyed when Jack appeared.

"So this is where you are," he said, somewhat crossly. "I have been looking all over for you. The next man is waiting for you."

I was upset that my manners had been bad. What would Mrs. T. say? What would she tell Mother?

"I am so sorry, Jack," I said, and then I smiled at the Neorealist. "Thank you very much. I've had a lovely time."

Jack nodded curtly to the Neorealist, gripped my arm firmly, and led me away. "Don't for heaven's sake fall for him," he said. "He is not the right person for you."

"Why, what's wrong with him?" I asked.

"He's pretty wild," answered Jack. "I only had him on the card because I knew the girl he was bringing down from New York, and we exchanged dances. Come on, here is George Aiken from Philadelphia, Miss Russell."

And so off I went onto the vast crowded floor of the gymnasium again, this time to the tune "There Are Smiles That Make You Happy, There Are Smiles That Make You Blue." Mr. Aiken was an inspired dancer, and we danced cheek to cheek, dipping and swaying to the enchanting tune. I closed my eyes, as I had seen the other girls doing, and abandoned myself to the joy of the moment.

At the end of the dance, when we returned to our starting point, there was the Neorealist with his partner, smiling and talking, much to Jack's annoyance. The next day I had a telephone call from him, and a great triple bunch of violets, which—sopping wet—I stuck into my belt and wore proudly all day. I felt that Jack and Mrs. T. thought the whole thing rather common. In fact, I myself felt quite fast; nevertheless, I was getting out of the prom just what I had wanted. All of Princeton would not drown itself for me, as Oxford did for Zuleika, but if one undergraduate got even his feet wet, I could return to De Sales Street in semitriumph at least.

I was reticent when I got home to Washington, for some reason. I did not want to discuss my adventure with family and friends. I described the girls' dresses, the music, the men (how Mother and her friends laughed at my use of the word), but I never mentioned the Neorealist. If I had I might also have had to mention the fact that I had passed myself off as being almost eighteen.

A few days after my return, a package arrived for me, special delivery, from New York. It was a beautifully bound copy of *The Oxford Book of English Verse,* lovely blue leather tooled in gold. On the flyleaf in very beautiful handwriting it said, "For Brooke Russell in the hope that we will read this book together"—and it was signed with his name.

I immediately sat down at Mother's desk and, taking a sheet of her very best notepaper, started my letter in my most Grown-up handwriting: "My very dear Mr. L."—having no idea that I was writing to the man I would marry before the year was out. From then on the patchwork took on another design.

Chapter 18

A
Family
Note

A genealogical tree makes pretty dull reading, but for those readers who would like to know a little about my forebears—

My mother's mother, Roberta Brooke McGill Howard (Granny to me), considered herself one of the "bluebloods of America." She often spoke of an ancestor, Daniel Carroll, who lived in Ireland and who, according to an ancient document, sent "20 of his sons accoutred in habiliments of war to serve in the interests of Charles the First." Other relatives of hers, after settling in America, returned to England to attend Eton and Cambridge, and in the middle of the eighteenth century one chose to pursue his studies in Lisbon. In other words, they were "quality," as Granny said, and I should always remember that and hold my head high. A certain Charles Carroll died childless, but on his deathbed requested that the children of his sister, Mary Clare Carroll McCubbin, should take his name. This they did, thereby inheriting his places, The Caves and Mount Clare. (Mount Clare exists to this day in Baltimore and is a charming house and a "historical monument" open to the public.) Nicholas McCubbin Carroll had a daughter, Mary Clare, who married Captain Robert Trail Spence, my great-grandfather. He was, by all accounts, a most gallant and intrepid fellow. A family legend has it that in 1804 in Tripoli when the cannon he was manning would not fire, he leaped astride it and, pulling out the cannonball with his bare hands, hurled it vigorously in the direction of the enemy. He must have done something more practical, for Stephen Decatur was so impressed with him that he wrote to Robert's father: "Your son has displayed a manliness of conduct that will make every American proud of him as a countryman."

This gallant and dedicated young officer rose rapidly in his profession and at the age of twenty-seven was a captain, the highest-ranking officer in the Navy. As senior officer of the Navy in 1821 he made what was called a "Manly protest in reply to a Proclamation of Francisco Morales, General-in-Chief of the Spanish forces on the Main, threatening with imprisonment

(previous page)
Father and Mother with Charles Lindbergh in front of their home in Haiti. When Father was high commissioner, Lindbergh flew down to Port-au-Prince at the time he was starting to work for Pan American Airways

and death all foreigners found in the Spanish Colonies whose countries were at war with Spain." "The conduct of Captain Spence," said a leading writer of the day, "has been honorable to humanity and the country which gave him birth. His noble, manly and dignified protest does him great honor and will be read by Americans with pleasure." The poor captain, alas, must have worn himself out by all these manly actions on land and sea, because he died at the age of thirty-two, leaving nine children.

One of his sons, the Honorable Carroll Spence, also tangled with the Turks, but on an amicable basis. He was appointed minister to the Sublime Porte by President Pierce in 1854, and under very difficult and extraordinary circumstances made the first treaty ever concluded between the United States and Persia. A New York paper, speaking of him, said: "Mr. Spence has represented this country near the Sublime Porte during an exciting period of European politics and has proved himself a diplomatist of no little ability. His powerful protest in behalf of the unfortunate Greeks at the commencement of the war induced the Turkish Ministry to rescind their harsh measures against them and obtained for him the thanks of every lover of humanity."

This relative I have always felt very close to. His portrait, painted in Constantinople by a Turkish artist, hung over the mantelpiece in Granny's downstairs sitting room, the Green Room, in Washington. It was painted in gouache and shows him in diplomatic uniform standing between two dragomen with red fezzes on their heads. All three of them have exactly the same faces, which always fascinated me. Before them is a table on which lies a document—the famous treaty, I imagine.

As I have said, my maternal grandmother was Roberta Brooke McGill. My great-grandfather, Oliver McGill, was a member of the legislature in Maryland but otherwise not a very serious character. He loved women and horses and bourbon. My great-grandmother and he had a place called Stranchia in the

Green Spring Valley, but the Civil War nearly ruined them because their slaves ran away and the place was not worked. They had two daughters, Lily, who married at an early age, and my grandmother Roberta, who was the beauty of the family and a great belle but who remained "on the vine," so to speak, flirting and dancing and refusing suitable young men. Her parents were naturally annoyed by this uncooperative behavior and sent her to Baltimore to stay with a gay and fashionable young married cousin. This gambit was not a success, however, as they soon found out that this charming lady was having an affair with a married man. Granny was quickly brought back to the country, where she languished, with no beaux at all.

Then my grandfather, George Henry Howard, appeared on the scene. There has always seemed something faintly mysterious about why he came to America from England with his brother William and his mother. The mother stayed long enough to establish her sons in law practice in Baltimore and to have them introduced into Good Society. Then she returned to England. My grandfather soon became a social success. He was good-looking, well educated, a beautiful dancer, and a very natty dresser, given to colored waistcoats and fancy watch fobs. He also played the piano and sang. His only drawback was that he had no private fortune. Granny, however, lost her head completely. She must have her "Mr. Howard" or she would pine away and die.

Actually, they were totally unsuited. Grandfather was an intellectual and basically serious, while Granny was a typical Southern belle wanting mad admiration and never opening a book except a light and romantic novel. Anyway, compatible or not, they were married in St. Thomas's, Garrison Forest, and went to live in Washington, where my grandfather entered into the practice of law. Granny's family bought them a rambling brick house on G Street with a large garden, and they proceeded to produce six children in ten years. One of the children, Little George, died in infancy. In afteryears when he was mentioned Granny would say, "Drat the child, I can't even remember his name." Granny hated having so many children and so little money but, halfway through the raising of this family, my grandfather did something unforgivable. He went to England on a visit (he went every two years) and when he came home he announced that he had returned to the faith of his fathers—he had become a Roman Catholic. This seemed a most terrible thing to Granny, who felt that Catholicism was the religion of servants and laborers (even though the Carroll relatives were Catholic). When Grandfather stated that he wished the children to be educated in Catholic schools, Granny fought it tooth and nail, but finally had to give in. The four girls went to the Sacred Heart Convent at Torresdale, outside of Philadelphia, and my uncle went to Georgetown. None of them became Catholic. In fact, after the rows that took place every Sunday at home, they seldom set foot in a church. So, in a way, Granny won, which is rather sad as the children all missed the joy and comfort of a spiritual life.

Grandfather, upon reentering the church, had received four lovely family portraits, which he brought from England. Granny hated all the Howards and refused to acknowledge their presence on the dining-room walls. I inherited one of them, but I never knew who the rosy-faced gentleman in the buff waistcoat was, and when he disappeared (years later) during a move from 1 Gracie Square to 10 Gracie Square, I could not have cared less. Now I am sorry for the departure of this mysterious ancestor and would like to have tracked him down.

My mother and all her sisters adored their father. He it was who controlled the life of the home. He wrote plays, made scenery, and had them and their friends act. He taught them Bach chorales and Gilbert and Sullivan, and made them memorize long passages of Shakespeare and Milton. Besides the plays he wrote for them, he wrote a play that reached the stage—*Tyrrel, A Tragedy*—in 1874 (it was a dreadful flop); *Deborah Blake,* a novel, in 1889; and *Things Seen and Heard,* in 1894.

My grandmother was thoroughly bored by his literary efforts. One of her relatives had married a Lowell from Boston and, by doing so, had become a damyankee and taboo, but Grandfather had a real affinity to these Boston Brahmins. They were a tremendous resource for him. Letters flew back and forth between 1800 G Street, Washington, and 68 Beacon Street, Boston. He poured out his dreams and aspirations and they, in turn, encouraged and applauded. Mary Lowell Putnam was particularly enthusiastic and seemed to spot in Grandfather a bit of genius, which unfortunately was not really there.

Overpowered by Grandmother's grand manners and her claims to more "lines" in the Colonial Dames than anyone else, my father was almost furtive about his family but they, too, were well educated and people of some substance.

Great-grandfather Russell was a gentleman farmer who lived at Rockville, Maryland, but Grandfather Russell chose the Navy as his career. When the Civil War broke out, though a Southerner and despite the fact that all his ties and affections were in the South, he was one of two officers who remained loyal to the Union and soon had the chance to show his mettle. He was aboard the U.S.S. frigate *Colorado* in September 1861, when men were asked to volunteer for a "cutting-out expedition." ("Cutting out" is a naval term signifying "to seize and carry off a vessel from a harbor or from under the guns of an enemy." Grandfather's expedition met with resistance as he boarded and was also under fire from the guns on shore.)

Admiral Porter, in his *Naval History of the United States,* writes: "Nearly one-fifth of the boarding party were either killed or wounded but the regrets that were felt for the loss of the gallant fellows who fell were somewhat compensated for (in the minds of the sailors) by the fact that their comrades had met the death of brave men fighting for the country they loved better than their lives."

Porter goes on to say: "This was without doubt the most gallant cutting-out affair that occurred during the war."

Grandfather was proclaimed a hero. I shall not continue with his career. Suffice it to say that he was a credit to the Navy abroad (he went with Perry to Japan) and at home. He ended up as rear admiral and retired in August 1886 to live in Washington.

In his forties he married my grandmother, May Treadwell, from Oswego, New York. A graduate of Miss Emma Willard's Seminary for Young Ladies at Troy, New York, she was from all accounts a member of a pious and gentle family. Her father was a minister, but ministers being notoriously poor they must have had some other income. She spent a year in Europe with an aunt and came home with a sketchbook filled with watercolors of an Italian spring and a trunkful of Roman sashes and spangled shawls and fans painted with scenes of Naples. She amalgamated these treasures with the Satsuma vases and Chinese Lowestoft Grandfather had received as gifts during his visits to the Orient and these lares and penates eventually all became ours.

Grandfather and Grandmother Russell had three children—two girls and finally, ten years later in answer to their prayers, my father, John Henry Russell, Jr. If Grandfather had done nothing else in his life but produce my father *I* would feel that he could rest on his laurels. Father had all the qualities of loyalty and courage and integrity in which his forebears seemed to have excelled but, at the same time, he was fun. He was a "merry saint." My Russell grandparents died long before I was born, so I never knew them and could never thank them for Father.

Epilogue

From the moment that I wrote the words "My dear Mr. Kuser" my life changed. A year later, after my seventeenth birthday on March 30, I was married on April 12 at St. John's Church, Lafayette Square, Washington, D.C., to John Dryden Kuser. I had a large and glamorous wedding, complete with eight bridesmaids, a maid of honor, eight ushers, and a best man. Mother had invited, besides my own friends, a host of hers, including the famous Alice Roosevelt Longworth, who commented on my jewelry. "You are competing with Mrs. Belmont, Brooke," she said laughingly to me. (Mrs. Belmont, having left her husband, Mr. Sloane, in order to marry Mr. Belmont, who had adorned her with ropes of pearls and a diamond-studded dog collar, was the talk of Washington, where they had come to live.)

Dryden and I were off to a supposedly marvelous honeymoon, but for me it was a nightmare from the start. All that I wrote in my diaries about Russian peasants, my flirtatious jottings and cries of spent passion were of course inventions. I did not know how flirting eventually ends, and when I found out I was shocked. I have written all about that in *Footprints*, so I won't go into it here. I can only think, on looking back, that I must have had a strong constitution and, also without knowing it, confidence enough in myself to feel I could eventually make my own life from this mockery of love. I must have looked back and remembered what the priests in Peking had said—that trees could continue to grow even after losing their branches in a storm. I did what they did. I lived through eight years of storms and sullen words, and even blows, and still felt strong enough in my roots to put out my shoots, just as the trees did.

I was rewarded by a second marriage of twenty years that made me stronger still. It was full of love, companionship, and the sheer joy of living. After the death of my adored husband, Charles Henry Marshall, I thought I would never marry again, but a year later I did. With Vincent Astor I led a very private, peaceful life, and when he died, he left me the Vincent Astor Foundation. It has been a wonderful thing for me. "You are going to have a hell of a lot of fun running it," he said, and it has certainly been more than that. I have returned money to New York City, where it was made by the original John Jacob Astor. In returning it, I have never let the foundation give to anything I did not see for myself, and in doing that, have seen what New York needs and tried to help as much as possible. I hope that we have helped to contribute to the city, giving as we do to both its strongest institutions and its weakest—in other words, from the cultural side of New York to the betterment of housing and to the education not only of children but also of adults.

It fills me with joy and gladness to have been able to contribute and I hope that I will leave the foundation with a good reputation of attending to New York's needs. I never thought I would have such extraordinary luck. I often wonder if my old friends in the Temple of One Hundred Courtyards know what their little girl has been doing and if we will ever meet again.

Me at age twenty-two with my baby Tony.